IMAGES

MW00981259

HISTORIC
NORTH END
HALIFAX

PAUL ERICKSON

NIMBUS
PUBLISHING

Copyright © Paul Erickson, 2004

All rights reserved. No part of this book may be reproduced, stored in a retrieval system or transmitted in any form or by any means without the prior written permission from the publisher, or, in the case of photocopying or other reprographic copying, permission from Access Copyright, 1 Yonge Street, Suite 1900, Toronto, Ontario M5E 1E5.

Nimbus Publishing Limited
PO Box 9166
Halifax, NS B3K 5M8
(902) 455-4286

Printed and bound in Canada

Design: Terri Strickland
Front cover: Coaling HMS *Ariadne*, c.1898
Title page: Traces of Fort Needham Redoubt, c.1920s, NSARM

Library and Archives Canada Cataloguing in Publication

      Erickson, Paul A.
      Historic North End Halifax / Paul Erickson.
      Includes bibliographical references.
      ISBN 1-55109-498-3

1. North End (Halifax, N.S.)—History. 2. North End (Halifax, N.S.)—History—Pictorial works. 3. Halifax (N.S.)—History. 4. Halifax (N.S.)—History—Pictorial works. I. Title.

FC2346.52.E753 2004   971.6'225   C2004-905956-4

We acknowledge the financial support of the Government of Canada through the Book Publishing Industry Development Program (BPIDP) and the Canada Council for our publishing activities.

 *Dedication*

To Halifax North Enders

Contents

Preface

This book is an illustrated history of the North End of Halifax, Nova Scotia. To create the book, I defined chapters, selected chapter illustrations, grouped the illustrations into themes, and wrote text for each theme. As a result, the text and illustrations work in tandem, complementing one another. Viewers can thumb through the book, locate engaging illustrations, then read the accompanying text, or, preferably, because the texts constitute a narrative, users can read and view the book simultaneously from beginning to end. Either way, the introduction provides a concise summary.

The book is a labour of love, and numerous individuals and institutions helped me do the necessary work. Former publisher Dorothy Blythe and sales manager Dan Soucoup of Nimbus Publishing invited me to undertake the project, and managing editor Sandra McIntyre, production manager Heather Bryan, and other members of the Nimbus team skillfully shepherded it through to completion. By granting me a sabbatical leave of absence from teaching, Saint Mary's University provided the requisite time. The key research and writing was done in fall 2003 and early winter 2004, almost all of it at Nova Scotia Archives and Records Management. The archives is a wonderful repository of information, and I thoroughly enjoyed parking myself there for several weeks. While there, I benefitted from the expert and efficient help of senior archivist Garry Shutlak, archivist Philip Hartling, receptionist Kelly Schlay, and archival assistants Darlene Brine, Virginia Clark, George Dupuis, Gail Judge, Barry Smith, and Anjali Vohra. At the Maritime Command Museum, director Marilyn Gurney generously allowed me access to valuable holdings, as did curatorial assistant Lynne-Marie Richard at the Maritime Museum of the Atlantic. I received additional help and information from Henry Bishop, curator of the Black Cultural Centre for Nova Scotia; John Langley, president of the Cunard Steamship Society; William Nycum, president of William Nycum & Associates Limited; Karen De Young of Larex Properties; Bill Campbell, Katie Cottreau-Robins, Dawn Erickson, George Fong, Bruce Stewart, and Paul Williams.

Crucial to the success of a book such as this are its illustrations. The reproduction quality of some illustrations is unavoidably sub-optimal, but these illustrations are valuable, so I have nevertheless used them. Although I credit all illustrations at the end of the book, I credit them again here: City of Toronto Archives, CRM Group, Maritime Command Museum, Maritime Museum of the Atlantic, National Archives of Canada, Nova Scotia Archives and Records Management, William Nycum & Associates, Katie Cottreau-Robins, George Fong, Owen Lane, John Langley, Dan Soucoup, Elizabeth Stevens, and Paul Williams. I thank all of these people and institutions for their assistance.

The book is full of facts, names, dates, and numbers, some of which I have generalized, estimated, or approximated. Readers who would like to explore my sources, or simply learn more, can consult the list of references. Some of my information was recalled from earlier research, writing, and teaching, as well as living in the North End for more than twenty years.

It is a daunting responsibility to characterize a past that has involved tens of thousands of people. In discharging that responsibility, I have endeavoured to be accurate, but, in a book with so many details, it is almost inevitable that some inaccuracies will have crept in. I apologize for any inaccuracies in advance and assure readers and viewers that they were unintentional. As an author, I am an outsider telling a story about other people's lives. It is likely that my story and these people's own stories will, to some extent, differ. Acknowledging these differences, my goal is to maximize opportunities for viewers and readers to forge their own meaningful connections to the past. If I succeed, however imperfectly, I will consider my effort worthwhile.

Paul A. Erickson
Halifax, Nova Scotia
February 2004

Historic North End Halifax

Halifax is a collection of neighbourhoods. These neighbourhoods arise from geography, patterns of settlement, and social attitudes. Geography divides Halifax into a peninsula, settled first, and a mainland, most of it settled much later. When Haligonians think about the peninsula, they commonly divide it into downtown and the North, South, and West Ends. Downtown is midway along the eastern side, facing Halifax harbour, while the North End extends to Bedford Basin and the South End extends to the Northwest Arm and Point Pleasant Park. The West End is the northwest quadrant of the peninsula, bordering the isthmus that links it to the mainland.

Because these regions are states of mind as well as geography, Haligonians are prone to debate their boundaries, especially Haligonians proud of where they live. Most Haligonians would agree that the boundaries of the South End are downtown, Citadel Hill, the Halifax Common, and Quinpool Road, a boundary common with the West End. Meanwhile, the boundaries of the North End are downtown, Citadel Hill, the Halifax Common, and Robie (in some places Windsor) Street, another boundary common with the West End. A popular stereotype is that the South End is upperclass, the West End middleclass, and the North End lowerclass. This stereotype is inaccurate. Of the three, the North End developed first and is, arguably, the most diverse and culturally rich part of Halifax. The story of how it got that way begins more than 250 years ago.

Origin of the North Suburbs

In June 1749, Colonel Edward Cornwallis and some 2,500 settlers sailed into Halifax harbour to establish the British colonial town of Halifax, named after the Earl of Halifax, Chief Lord of Trade and Plantations. The function of the town was strategic, to counter the French presence at Louisbourg, so Cornwallis chose a site on the slope of Citadel Hill where ships could anchor safely and enjoy protection from a hilltop fort. Except for traces of Mi'kmaw encampment, the colonists encountered dense forest running down to the water. Almost immediately, they began clearing the forest of trees and fashioning a rectangular grid of streets and blocks with building lots. Today this grid remains essentially intact, bounded on the east by Water Street, the south by Salter and Blowers streets, the west by Brunswick Street, and the north by Scotia Square.

Because the British considered the French and Mi'kmaq hostile, they surrounded the town with a wooden palisade incorporating five perimeter forts. The north forts were Fort Luttrell, near the northeast corner of Citadel Hill, and Fort Grenadier, near what is now the Cogswell Interchange. East of Fort Grenadier was the north town gate, outside the gate a narrow strip of cleared land, and then—wilderness.

Anticipating that the French and Mi'kmaw threat outside the palisades would subside, surveyor Charles Morris created north and south suburbs. The north suburbs extended toward North Street, the south suburbs toward South Street. In the north suburbs, to allow gardens that would help feed the town, he created lots that were much larger than those inside the palisades. Initially, the only road into the north suburbs was Water Street skirting the harbour. At the time, there was no north Barrington Street, and north Brunswick and Gottingen streets were fledgling country lanes leading to scattered log cabins. With this limited infrastructure in place, the old north suburbs—the original North End—was ready to receive its first influx of inhabitants.

Arrival of Foreign Protestants

Life in early Halifax was challenging and harsh. To ease the burden of colonists, the British Crown encouraged the immigration of so-called foreign Protestants. These foreigners were residents of Germany, France, and Switzerland who came to Halifax indentured to individuals or government. A few foreign Protestants accompanied Cornwallis in 1749, and between 1750 and 1752, approximately 2,500 more arrived, enduring grueling voyages plagued by death and disease. The new settlers almost doubled the population of the town. They went to work on fortifications and public facilities, contributing significantly to the construction of early Halifax.

The majority of foreign Protestants settled in the north suburbs, building modest wooden cottages. These cottages sprang up along Brunswick and Gottingen streets, named for German locations, and also along Lockman Street, the predecessor of north Barrington, named after Leonard Lockman, a prominent German immigrant. Soon there were so many Germans in the north suburbs that, following Anglicization, the area became known as Dutch (*Deutsche*) Town.

In 1753, governor Peregrine Thomas Hopson relocated most of the German settlers to Lunenburg. A few remained in Halifax, and a few more trickled back, and this nucleus kept the German tradition alive. Some of the early Dutch cottages survived for two centuries, and German vestiges persisted in the North End in names, not only of streets, but also of families, such as the Schwartz family, founder of Schwartz & Sons, manufacturer of spices.

At Brunswick and Gerrish streets, surveyor Morris reserved a special lot for a German burial ground and church. In 1756, German residents moved a barn to this location and converted it into a church, four years later enlarging the church and adding a steeple. This church—the Little Dutch Church—was the first Lutheran church in Canada. Almost 250 years later, it remains in its original location, surrounded on two sides by graves that bear old German names. The Little Dutch Church is the second oldest building in Halifax. A humble place of worship, it evokes an era when this part of the North End was essentially a frontier between the town and virgin trees.

The Naval Dockyard

Along Halifax harbour north of downtown is an obscured promontory once called Gorham's Point. Located at the foot of Gerrish Street, the point took its name from New Englander Joseph Gorham, leader of Gorham's Rangers, who helped protect

Halifax from the Mi'kmaq and the French. In 1759, the Royal Navy bought some of Gorham's property for a new naval dockyard. With Halifax so strategically located, it was important to be able to maintain and repair naval vessels in the harbour. A core installation at the dockyard was the careening wharf, where ships were hoisted out of water, inspected, and their hulls fixed.

Soon the Navy enclosed the dockyard with a fence and a gate at the foot of Artz Street, then called Naval Yard Lane. In 1783, alarmed at the possibility of importing contagious diseases, it built a naval hospital along the water north of Gorham's Point. The dockyard expanded steadily south of the hospital and north of the point, and by 1815 it comprised more than seventy-five buildings and wharves—a city within a city and an economic boon to the North End.

The dockyard converted north Water Street into a thoroughfare between the dockyard and the town. Businesses and wharves along the street serviced the dockyard, as did area farms, which provided livestock and crops. Expanding the infrastructure of Dutch Town, workers moved up the hill to Lockman, Brunswick, and other intersecting streets. In Halifax, high-ranking naval officers have always belonged to the social elite, so when in 1814 the Navy built a residence for its admiral on north Gottingen Street, the street became a residential address of distinction. In 1819, after defeats in the American War of Independence and the War of 1812, Britain relocated most of its Atlantic naval fleet from Halifax to Bermuda. Although the North End suffered, the navy subsequently revived and loomed large in the first and second world wars.

The Military Garrison

Halifax developed in an era of British, French, and American international conflicts. The first wave of hostilities ended when Britain expelled Acadians in 1755 and then achieved victories over France at Louisburg in 1758 and Quebec in 1759. Afterwards, although tension with France resurfaced, Britain refocused its attention on its restless North American colonies, thirteen of which, excepting Nova Scotia, declared independence in 1776. During the seven-year American War of Independence, Halifax earned its reputation as Warden of the North by helping stage the British naval campaign. The dockyard swelled with activity, the population of the town soared, and Halifax overflowed with Loyalist refugees. During the War of 1812, this cycle repeated itself, leaving Halifax, as it started, a town whose primary purpose was to serve the strategic interests of the Crown.

Halifax is a city by the sea, but, in the beginning, it was also vulnerable from land. The locations of the town and dockyard were challenging, because they required defense of a harbour that afforded opportunity for enemies to seize the opposite shore. Several fortifications, including Citadel Hill, stood guard against such attempts. Halifax was also exposed to attack from the rear, where troops could cross the peninsular isthmus and make their way toward town. During the American War of Independence, there were two peninsular roads: Windsor Street, the oldest road outside of town, and Lady Hammond Road, connected to north

Gottingen Street. Much of the land enclosed by these roads was open farmland, relatively easy to both attack and defend.

Early on, Colonel Cornwallis had protected the isthmus with blockhouses, but the new dockyard required a second line of landward defense. In 1775, Commanding Royal Engineer Colonel William Spry expropriated North End properties for fortifications. Outside the north and south ends of the dockyard, near the feet of North and Gerrish streets, he built two blockhouses, and up the hill, along Brunswick Street, at intersections with North, Gerrish, and Artz streets, he built three bastions. Within the dockyard itself, on top of a hillock near North Street, he built Fort Coote. Despite all this protection, the dockyard was still open to attack from a hill one half mile northwest of Fort Coote. There Spry expropriated almost nine acres and constructed an armed earthen redoubt–Fort Needham. From Fort Needham, the British could detect and interdict any American advance along Lady Hammond Road, Gottingen Street, or, farther afield, Windsor Street.

The history of Halifax is a boom and bust cycle of war-driven prosperity followed by post-war recession and decline. This is especially true for the North End, which, besides the dockyard, became home to military barracks, magazines, armouries, hospitals, and churches scattered along the route from Fort Needham to Citadel Hill. During the American War of Independence, all North End naval and military installations were on alert. None was engaged in battle, and after the war they fell into disuse and disrepair. In anticipation of the War of 1812, they were rehabilitated and two blockhouses were added, one at the north end of Needham Hill and another, Fort McAlpine, on a hill at Windsor Street and Lady Hammond Road. After the war, these too deteriorated. Halifax then embarked on a century of relative peace, during which time it had to learn how to reinvent itself as something other than a British armed camp.

Gradual Expansion North

Between the War of 1812 and the First World War, except for military preparedness, most of the economy in Halifax was homegrown. In the early part of this period, the population increased mainly in the North End. In 1820, there were only a few houses along south Gottingen Street, to the west of which lay Creighton's and Maynard's fields. The area north of North Street was still farmland, much of it owned by families of German and other original land grantees. Along Windsor Street there were a few inns, and north of Almon Street stretched Willow Park, a large experimental farm created by horticulturalist John Young. By 1841, Halifax was officially incorporated as a town, and by the 1850s its water supply was a chain of lakes on the mainland, pushing its first line of defense off the peninsula. At the same time, new breech-loading ordnance replaced smooth-bore cannon, rendering old fortifications, including Citadel Hill, obsolete. Tax-exempt military property littered the city, superseded in importance by the property of a new breed of mercantile merchant entrepreneurs, many of whom prospered in the West Indies trade. This was Nova Scotia's Age of Sail—its golden Bluenose Era.

At the time of incorporation, the population of Halifax exceeded 14,000. More than 400 of its 2,300 residences were located in the old north suburbs, many of them on a honeycomb of quaint streets fringing downtown. The most prestigious street in the North End—and in Halifax—soon became Brunswick Street, which boasted spacious lots, a harbour view, and escape from a crowded, commercializing downtown. Brunswick Street filled with landmark churches and Georgian and Victorian mansions, and houses began to occupy Creighton's and Maynard's fields. On Gottingen Street north of North Street, Admiralty House spurred construction of elaborate villas with wrought-iron gates and carriage lanes. Meanwhile, south of the sprawling dockyard, the harbour was crowded with businesses and wharves, foremost among them the headquarters of shipping magnate Samuel Cunard.

At this time, Halifax experienced an influx of Irish immigrants, who soon constituted one third of the population. Most of the Irish settled south of downtown, where the near south suburbs became Irish Town, contrasted with Dutch Town to the north. Because Halifax was still pre-industrial, unlike in American cities, the Irish and other ethnic populations were not forced into the urban proletariat, and they did not experience as much discrimination. Therefore, Halifax failed to develop a conspicuous European ethnic "inner city." The absence of large ethnic enclaves characterized the North End before railways and industry caused it to transform physically and socially.

Impact of Railways

In the mid-nineteenth century, industrializing nations encouraged the construction of passenger and freight railways. Before Canadian confederation, the Nova Scotia Railway completed a line around the tip of Halifax peninsula terminating in a depot at the foot of Duffus Street. The depot opened in 1854. The rail line followed the route of Campbell Road, which had been built sixteen years earlier and promoted the growth of Campbell Town, later called Richmond. The Richmond depot served all of Halifax two miles to the south. In 1866, a horse-drawn street railway began transporting freight and passengers between Halifax and the depot. Campbell Road, Upper Water Street, and Barrington Street were then discontinuous. In 1871, to eliminate this inconvenience, Halifax made the streets continuous, creating the north Barrington Street of today and knitting the North End together.

After Canadian confederation, the Intercolonial Railway took over the rail line and started extending it from Halifax to the Great Lakes. In the North End, it extended the rail line south to a new, grander depot at the foot of North Street, opened in 1877. It continued to extend the line south through the old dockyard to new Deep Water terminals, which were able to accommodate larger vessels than in the shallower waters of Richmond. All this construction spurred enlargement, upgrading, and demolition of old wharves along Upper Water Street. The Intercolonial wanted to extend the line still farther south to downtown, but this move was prohibitively disruptive and expensive. Instead, the city authorized construction of a new rail line blasted through bedrock along the West and South ends to terminals near Point Pleasant Park. This route was completed around the time of the First World War.

Meanwhile, back in the North End, the Intercolonial constructed a spur line from Bedford Basin southward along flat land to the vicinity of Young Street, Robie Street, and Kempt Road. This line allowed manufactured goods to be transported to the harbour for export, creating, in effect, an industrial park. Even the first two bridges across Halifax harbour were extensions of the railway.

The new railways had a dramatic impact on the North End. Besides obvious physical changes, they triggered alteration of residential neighbourhoods, notably on Brunswick Street, where smoke and noise from the new North Street station caused the wealthy elite to relocate to more genteel streets in the South End. More significantly, the railway provided infrastructure for industry, which proliferated in the North End, promoting its reputation as blue collar.

Promise of Industry

At first, the railways were slow in spurring the Halifax economy, because traditional Nova Scotian exports such as lumber and fish were available more cheaply in Upper Canada. Then, in 1879, the Dominion government subsidized Nova Scotian industry with protective national tariffs, and industrialization accelerated. Merchant money quickly converted to industrial capital, and new industries sprang up in the North End, most of them centred on Richmond, which spread westward beyond Robie toward Windsor Street.

Prominent among North End industries were the Nova Scotia Sugar Refinery, located along Intercolonial Railway tracks at the foot of Kaye Street, and the Nova Scotia Cotton Company, located on thirty acres of land west of Robie Street and Young. Capitalized with $600,000, these industries employed hundreds of workers, and, at ten storeys, the refinery was the tallest building in Canada east of Montreal. Near the refinery were the Gunn and Company milling plant, the Halifax Graving Dock, and Hillis and Sons Foundry, manufacturer of furnaces and stoves. Near the Cotton Company were Nova Scotia Paint Works and Nova Scotia Car Works, manufacturer of railway cars. South of Richmond, in the old north suburbs, companies manufactured goods ranging from coffee, spices, and beer, to glassware, carriages, and pianos. By 1900, owing largely to industry, the North End boasted more than half of the assessed property valuation in Halifax.

While most industrial capitalists lived in the South End, the vast majority of industrial workers lived in the North End. To house these workers, private developers built modest, two-storey dwellings around Richmond and beyond. West of Needham Hill, the Halifax Land Company created subdivisions with streets named after local families such as the Hennesseys and Merkels. On the eastern slope of Needham Hill, many of the older streets of Richmond had already developed in this manner. By the end of the century, Gottingen, Isleville, Agricola, and Robie extended north of Duffus Street and Lady Hammond Road. In a short span of two decades, Richmond had become a full-fledged industrial suburb and a vibrant community with its own schools and churches.

The promise of industry in Halifax was short-lived, its potential extinguished by events over which Haligonians had little control. Some local industries were undercapitalized and inexpertly managed, but the main reason they faltered was that the centre of Canadian population was moving westward to Ontario and Quebec, where iron, coal, and water to generate electricity were more abundant. As soon as Upper Canadian industries prospered, they outbid or bought out their competitors in Nova Scotia, forcing Halifax industry into decline. To make matters much worse, a revival of industry during the First World War was cut short by the catastrophic Halifax Explosion.

The Halifax Explosion

On the morning of December 6, 1917, Canada was engaged in a protracted war with Germany. Haligonians were accustomed to seeing the harbour packed with wartime vessels, so, at first, they paid little attention to the French munitions ship *Mont Blanc* and the Belgian relief ship *Imo* as they passed dangerously close to one another in the narrows at Richmond. Then the *Imo* collided with the *Mont Blanc*, setting it on fire and sending up huge plumes of black smoke. Richmond residents stopped to look at the burning ship, which, abandoned by its crew, drifted helplessly toward shore. At 9:05 AM, the *Mont Blanc*'s cargo of munitions ignited, unleashing the greatest man-made force before detonation of the atomic bomb.

Almost instantly, a deadly percussion wave swept up Needham Hill, levelling much of Richmond, pulverizing people with debris, and riveting them with shards of glass. The *Mont Blanc*'s anchor blew all the way to the Northwest Arm. The water receded, then released itself in a tidal wave that swept away waterfront buildings and wharves. Overturned stoves set wooden houses on fire, turning them into crematoria. Schools, churches, and factories collapsed, trapping hundreds. While Richmond bore the brunt of the explosion, throughout downtown and the South End windows shattered, plaster crumbled, and buildings cracked. The explosion was felt as far away as Truro. In a cruel twist of fate, the next day a fierce snowstorm set in, burying and freezing bodies and hampering rescue and relief. So horrifying was the carnage that one attending physician went insane and committed suicide. An estimated toll of the explosion was 2,000 people killed, 9,000 injured, and 6,000 homeless, with property damage exceeding $35 million. In statistical terms the explosion was more deadly than the famous Chicago fire and the San Francisco earthquake combined.

The tragedy of the Halifax Explosion was mitigated by examples of heroism, sacrifice, and generosity. People died while trying to pull others out of wreckage, and railway dispatcher Vincent Coleman died at his post while warning an incoming train. Relief money and supplies poured in from around the world, notably from Massachusetts and other New England States. But the reaction was also ugly. Acting on a rumour that the explosion was a German attack, Haligonians stoned residents with German surnames, and anti-French sentiment, simmering over resistance to military conscription in Quebec, boiled over when Haligonians blamed the captain of the *Mont Blanc* for the fateful collision. This welter of emotions has made the Halifax Explosion almost legendary. If Canadians today know little else about the North End, they know that once upon a time it blew up.

Rebuilding the North End

Recovering from the Halifax Explosion required the intervention of the federal and provincial governments. In January 1918, to alleviate suffering and to rebuild, these governments created the Halifax Relief Commission. Largely circumventing municipal government, they gave the commission sweeping powers to expropriate property, clear away wreckage, build temporary housing, and redesign the North End.

For its redesign, the commission turned to Thomas Adams, town planner in Ottawa. Adams was an Englishman who promoted the vision of the "garden city," wherein cities incorporated green spaces reminiscent of the country. His design for the North End featured new streets, houses, and a showcase park. Recognizing that the steep parallel streets of Richmond were impractical, Adams designed two angled boulevards, Dartmouth and Devonshire avenues, to meet in an X-shaped civic centre. His design for new housing was two-pronged. West of Needham Hill, between Gottingen Street and Agricola, he designed the Hydrostone district, a series of short boulevards lined with row houses that looked "olde-English." The district took its name from a locally manufactured building stone, chosen to resist fire. Adams worried about the re-encroachment of industry, so he intended the Hydrostones, modest and relatively dense, to buffer more prestigious housing to the east. There, on the slope of Needham Hill, he designed a few large homes, hoping to seed private investment. He envisioned his park atop Needham Hill, taking advantage of its panoramic view.

Most of Adams's vision of the North End became reality. The Halifax Relief Commission built the angled streets, with Richmond School at their intersection and several old east-west streets shortened or eliminated. It completed the Hydrostones in 1921, rented them until 1948, and then sold them. Altogether, the commission built hundreds of homes in the North End, 350 of them Hydrostones and the rest of them scattered across Needham Hill and points west. In 1959, after spending $150,000 on beautification, the commission transferred Fort Needham Park to the city. At first, these efforts achieved only partial success. After the First World War, Halifax suffered a severe economic recession, followed a decade later by the Great Depression. Large areas of the North End retained physical scars of the explosion, and survivors, some superstitious, refused to move back. Hoped-for rejuvenation of former Richmond did not really take place until the Second World War, when Halifax regained people and a semblance of prosperity.

Saga of Africville

Black Haligonians have come to the city for a variety of reasons. In earliest days, they were bought and sold as slaves, and later, during the American War of

Independence, they arrived as slaves of British Loyalists. Some came as black Loyalists, especially following the War of 1812, and more came as freed or escaped slaves at the time of the American Civil War. Other black settlers came from Caribbean islands, notably the Maroons from Jamaica. All these settlers made Nova Scotia the province with the largest number of black residents in Canada, a record which it held until recently.

Some black settlers relocated to West Africa, but most ended up living in rural communities on the outskirts of Halifax, where the government granted them land only marginally suited for subsistence. Facing hardship, a few drifted back to Halifax, settling in the old north suburbs or at the northern tip of the peninsula in the isolated community of Africville.

The precise origins of Africville are unclear, but they date back to the nineteenth century, when the community probably served as a base of operations for the construction of Campbell Road. Close to Halifax, residents still enjoyed relative privacy and access to Bedford Basin, where they swam and fished. Africville began on 15 acres, and it never expanded much beyond this original size, so, as the population increased, the lots became smaller and more important to preserve through inheritance. The centre of the community was Seaview African United Baptist Church, which maintained social fabric and spirit. The Halifax Explosion spared most of Africville. Although challenged, the community persevered for another fifty years.

As Halifax expanded, it encroached upon Africville in ways that would have been intolerable elsewhere. The Intercolonial Railway line ran right through the community, necessitating demolition of some houses and operating within feet of others, leading to injuries and deaths. In 1860, Rockhead Prison was built on a bluff overlooking Africville, and a few years later it was joined by the Infectious Diseases Hospital. Over the years, added to these intrusions were huge power transmission towers and an oil storage tank, fertilizer manufacturing plant, coal-handling facility, slaughterhouse, and municipal dump.

In the mid-twentieth century, Africville became increasingly controversial. While many residents remained proud of their community, other Haligonians regarded it with apprehension or embarrassment. What to do about it became a topic of debate in municipal government. In the early 1940s, the government was preoccupied with the Second World War, but after the war, it approved plans that in the 1960s led to the relocation of Africville residents and the razing of their community. In retrospect, the manner in which this was done appears to have been unfair and heavy-handed, so the demise of Africville has kept controversy about it alive.

The Second World War

As in past wars, during the Second World War, Halifax swelled with people and purpose. It was a time of great anxiety and excitement. The city was united in cause, and effects of the war were everywhere, not only in newspapers and on radio, but in businesses and homes and on streets, where civilians mingled with men and women in uniform, straining city services to their limits. Despite battlefield horrors, Haligonians remain sentimental about this era and recall with pride their contributions to the war effort.

With its dockyard, piers, and shipbuilding facilities, as well as its cheaper residential accommodations, the North End bore the brunt, and reaped much of the benefit, of wartime expansion. At times, the dockyard employed more than 3,000 people, and Halifax Shipyards, built on the Halifax Graving Dock site, repaired and refitted more than 7,000 vessels. To house the necessary workforce, owners of nearby North End dwellings carved them up into flats, apartments, and rooms. As a result, the housing stock, already frayed from decades of use and neglect, deteriorated even more. In May 1945, following the announcement of German surrender, wartime frenzy and pent-up pressure erupted in Halifax's notorious V-E Day riots, a spree of celebratory vandalism and looting that began in the North End and proceeded downtown. Two months later, in July, ammunition at a magazine near Bedford exploded, causing panic among North Enders who feared, but fortunately did not experience, a second Halifax Explosion. Clearly it was time to settle down, welcome home troops, and build on peace.

During the war, the Canadian military erected temporary housing in Mulgrave Park and other open spaces around the North End. The largest open space was north of Duffus Street and Lady Hammond Road, where, beyond the reach of planner Thomas Adams, the area still comprised farms, former church property, and institutions encroaching Africville. Here developers erected small, single-family prefabricated bungalows—"prefabs"—to house wartime workers and returning servicemen and their families. Designed to last twenty years, these prefabs are still standing, attesting to their quality of construction and, on streets such as Vestry and Glebe, creating a homogeneous, almost suburban look. This building boom largely completed the residential settlement of Halifax's North End. In the post-war era, new building continued, but greater changes were wrought by the wrecking ball.

Urban Renewal

Even before the Second World War ended, civic leaders recognized that they had to renew an aging housing stock, infrastructure, and a neglected urban core. During the 1950s and 1960s, decades of optimism and rapid change, Halifax adopted a series of renewal plans, the most influential among them designed by "outside expert" Gordon Stephenson. These plans targeted the North End, the oldest, poorest, and most vulnerable part of the peninsula. With scattered community opposition, city council began implementing the plans, a process that transformed parts of the North End beyond recognition.

By 1955, the Angus L. Macdonald harbour bridge connected Dartmouth to Halifax at North Street. The main avenue from the bridge to downtown was Gottingen Street, then bustling with commerce. To maintain this commerce with automobiles, the city demolished buildings behind the stores on Gottingen Street to create parking lots. Enforcing a controversial building code, it demolished many more buildings around the old North End, rendering its appearance gap-toothed. Later, it filled some of these gaps with high-rise residences for senior citizens and elements of a model inner city called Uniacke Square.

For the North End shoreline, the city proposed Harbour Drive, a multi lane expressway modelled on the East Side Highway in New York. This scheme involved widening Barrington Street and linking it to widened east-west streets at elevated traffic interchanges, one of them at Cogswell Street. Urban planners judged the buildings on north Barrington Street "unworthy" of the main route to and from downtown, so the city demolished almost all of them south of North Street. Work on Harbour Drive began but was aborted when heritage-minded Haligonians prevented demolition of the waterfront buildings that became Historic Properties. Still, the plan for Harbour Drive left much of the old North End gutted.

The showpiece of renewed Halifax was Scotia Square, a complex of concrete high-rises designed to make the downtown modern. Scotia Square sits on a former honeycomb of quaint old streets and tenements, some of them dating back to the original downtown and north suburbs. The city razed this whole area, relocating many of its residents to new public housing farther north at Mulgrave Park. Scotia Square then became a centre of neighbourhood commerce, contributing to the economic decline of Gottingen Street.

The final major episode of renewal took place in Africville, by then a perceived affront to the social conscience of the city. Africville also occupied land that city planners eyed for new industry, and it stood in the way of the approach to the new A. Murray MacKay harbour bridge. Between 1964 and 1970, citing the desirability of racial integration, the city expropriated or purchased and then bulldozed Africville houses, moving some residents out on dump trucks. Today, the site of Africville is Seaview Park, where occasionally former residents have gathered to protest their removal and lament the loss of their community.

Despite these efforts, or partly because of them, between 1961 and 1976 the population of the North End declined forty-two percent, and enrolment at some schools dropped seventy-five percent. The drain of people to other areas, mainly suburbs, did not reverse itself until the oil shortages and hyper-inflation of the 1970s, when a new breed of resident moved in, and the North End began to "gentrify." Today, owing to urban renewal, new and old residents alike find much of North End physically disconnected from its past, making it important to reconnect through words and pictures, so that its past can be appreciated, as it so richly deserves.

Chapter 1

Origin of the North Suburbs

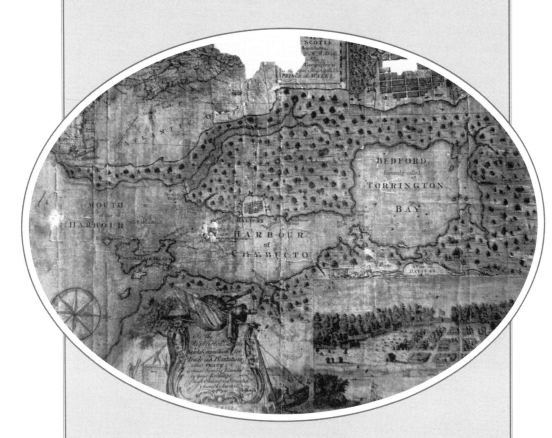

HALIFAX 1749-1750

A Clearing in the Forest

Halifax began amid epic struggles between Britain and France for colonial influence in North America. France had already established a nearby colony at Louisbourg. In 1745, Britain captured Louisbourg, then in 1748 ceded it back to France in the Treaty of Aix-la-Chapelle. In March 1749, Lord Halifax, president of the British Board of Trade, proposed protecting British interests in Nova Scotia by establishing a colony south of Louisbourg at Chebucto, his name for what the native Mi'kmaq called *Chebook-took*, "at the biggest harbour." Hurriedly, newspaper advertisements recruited settlers for an expedition of some 3,000 people led by Colonel Edward Cornwallis. The expedition arrived at Chebucto in June 1749, and proceeded to create the new colony, named after Lord Halifax.

Cornwallis situated Halifax on the eastern slope of a peninsula dominated by a sugarloaf hill, later called Citadel Hill, where ships could anchor safely and the colony could be protected from wind and both landward and seaward attack. The job of laying out the settlement belonged to engineer John Brewse and surveyor Charles Morris. Brewse planned the defenses of the settlement, while Morris planned its grid of streets and blocks with building lots. After a challenging first winter, most of the defenses and grid were in place.

In January 1750, to promote the new colony, Thomas Jefferys, geographer to the Prince of Wales, published a composite map of Halifax. In the upper left-hand corner is an inset map of Nova Scotia drawn by "Mons. D'Anville," geographer to the French King. In the upper and lower right-hand corners are modified versions of a plan and view drawn from a topmasthead by expeditioner Moses Harris, first published in October 1749. Harris possibly also drew the large centre map of Chebucto Harbour and environs.

The composite map shows Halifax as a clearing in the forest surrounded by a wooden palisade and five perimeter forts. In Harris's view, there are still no wharves, so ships are anchored offshore in the vicinity of George's Island. Some stumps of cleared trees remain, and there are both temporary tents and hastily constructed wooden dwellings. Noticeable in both the view and plan is the central rectangular Grand Parade with, in the plan, the location of St. Paul's Church erroneously marked by the letter C (the church was built the following year at the south rather than the north end of the parade.) Much of this depicted perpendicular street grid remains intact today in downtown Halifax, with George Street intersecting the Grand Parade at its centre (in the plan letter A), paralleled by Prince Street to the south (B) and Duke Street to the north (C). Perpendicular to these streets along the lengthier sides of the parade are Barrington Street to the east and Argyle Street to the west.

At this time, the North End was essentially wilderness beyond the north palisades and forts. Soon, however, the North End expanded and encroached upon two geographical features identified in the centre map. Bing's Beach, probably named after John Byng, officer in the Royal Navy and governor of Newfoundland, became the foot of Cornwallis Street, and Gorham's Point, named after Joseph Gorham (Goreham) or his brother John, became the foot of Gerrish Street. Especially important was Gorham's Point, which in 1759 became the site of the Royal Naval Dockyard.

Edward Cornwallis Revisits Halifax

Colonel Edward Cornwallis and his staff set sail for Chebucto on May 14, 1749, in the sloop-of-war *Sphinx*. Transport ships carrying 2,576 passengers and store ships with staff and military personnel set sail a few days later. The *Sphinx* took a more northerly route than the rest of the fleet and sighted Nova Scotia on June 14, but, because the crew was unfamiliar with the land and lacked reliable charts, it waited for a week before entering Chebucto on June 21, the true Halifax Natal Day. The rest of the fleet arrived five days later. Owing significantly to the installation of ship ventilators that maintained hygiene, only one passenger, a child, died on the voyage.

With a commission given him by King George II, Cornwallis replaced Paul Mascarene of Annapolis Royal as governor of Nova Scotia and set up a governing council. On July 24, he wrote to the Board of Trade with detailed plans for Halifax, and on August 20, he wrote again that lots had been drawn for building. Cornwallis was committed to the British mission and outspoken in his criticism of authorities for not providing the necessary resources. His health also suffered, so, not entirely reluctantly, he left Halifax in October 1752, and was succeeded by governor Peregrine Thomas Hopson. His subsequent career in the military was undistinguished, and he ended up as governor of Gibraltar.

EDWARD CORNWALLIS (1712/13–1776) ON THE REPLICATED *SPHINX*, 1924

In 1924, Halifax staged a grand carnival to celebrate the 175th anniversary of its founding. The carnival featured a pageant recreating the Cornwallis landing. On August 6, a replica of the *Sphinx*, built at HMC Dockyard, sailed up the Northwest Arm to South Street, where it dropped anchor and hauled in its sails. On board, among others, was Major Philip Edward Prideaux in the rôle of Cornwallis. The party disembarked and proceeded up the street to Dalhousie University, where Prideaux read the Cornwallis Royal Commission in the presence of Acadian and Mi'kmaw representatives. The pageant was witnessed by more than 10,000 spectators and made front page headlines the following day in the *Halifax Herald*.

A Secret Map

In 1755, a new war between Britain and France loomed, with important battlegrounds in North America. Tensions ran high following the British capture of Fort Beauséjour and expulsion of Nova Scotian Acadians. In November, British Admiral Edward Boscawen reported finding a map of Halifax hidden in a cake of soap in the chest of a French officer en route to Louisbourg. The map is attributed to François-Pierre de Rigaud de Vandreuil, a Halifax prisoner, and likely was preparation for an attack on the town.

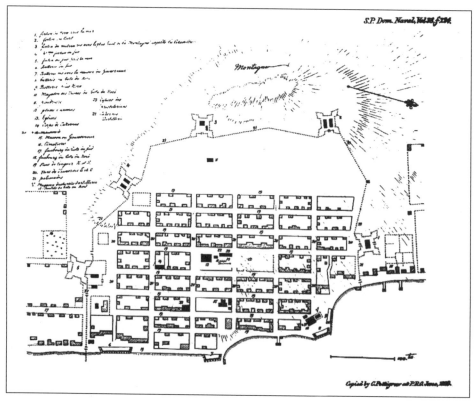

HALIFAX, 1755

The map shows in some detail the palisades (number 21) and five perimeter forts, with bastions and barracks (1–5). The north forts were Fort Luttrell (2) on the slope of Citadel Hill and Fort Grenadier (1) along the palisade near the water. Augmenting the forts were four shoreline batteries (6–9), two of which (8, 9) were near the old north suburbs. Behind the north batteries were two storehouses (10, V), which, with the batteries, formed a cluster of facilities that evolved into the ordnance yard.

The old north suburbs began at the north palisade and Fort Grenadier, where, as the map shows, there were wharves and buildings near the water and scattered uphill. Two parallel lines interrupting the dotted line of the north palisade mark the north gate of the town, which opened onto Upper Water Street, then running right along the water. In Halifax today, almost all land east of Water Street is artificial fill, which has concealed the original shoreline.

Laying Out the North Suburbs

In 1749, inside the palisades, surveyor Charles Morris created a grid of blocks most of which were 320 feet long and 120 feet wide (97.5 metres by 36.6 metres), with each block divided into building lots 40 feet long and 60 feet deep (12.2 metres by 18.3 metres). Outside the palisades, in the north suburbs extending to North Street and the south suburbs extending to South Street, Morris created larger lots to encourage farms and gardens that would help feed the town. The British Crown granted these lots to expedition members and new settlers on the condition that they be used. If they were not used, the Crown repossessed them and granted them to someone else. The original Crown grants mark the beginning of the chain of title to Halifax properties that extends to the present day.

In 1945, to aid property title research, H. Jackson prepared a series of maps of Halifax that identify the original Crown grantees, their lots, and some early property transactions. Jackson's map of the old north suburbs shows its early layout at a time when, owing to the presence of German settlers, it was known as Dutch (*Deutsche*) Town. Few of the lots had buildings, and many of the streets were only lanes, or paths, wandering through fields and woods. The original north suburbs began north of Wentworth (later Jacob) Street, just inside the original palisade with Fort Grenadier. The main routes toward North Street were Gottingen Street, Brunswick Street, and Water Street, which ran to, and along, the Naval Dockyard. Perpendicular to these streets, from south to north, were Hurd's Lane, Proctor's Lane, Cornwallis Street, Gerrish Street, and Naval Yard Lane (later Artz Street). Lockman Street, a predecessor of north Barrington Street, extended between North and Cornwallis.

Most of the lots between Hurd's Lane and Gerrish Street were relatively large, on the order of 100 x 250 feet (30.5 metres by 76.2 metres), while the lots between Gerrish Street and North Street were smaller, although still twice as large as most lots inside the palisades. The map shows a lot reserved for a Dutch church and cemetery at the intersection of Brunswick and Gerrish streets, and other lots in the north suburbs bear the names of prominent Halifax pioneers, such as Leonard Lockman, Joseph Gerrish, and John Gorham (Naval Yard). Other maps show water lots granted for wharves and commercial installations. This layout of the old north suburbs served as infrastructure for later expansion.

Halifax Prepares for War

In 1758, three years into renewed war with France, Halifax prepared to launch a major assault on Louisbourg and then Quebec. In the spring, General James Wolfe arrived with 41 warships, 120 transports, and some 12,000 troops. For weeks, the town teemed with activity as the force assembled provisions and rehearsed battle

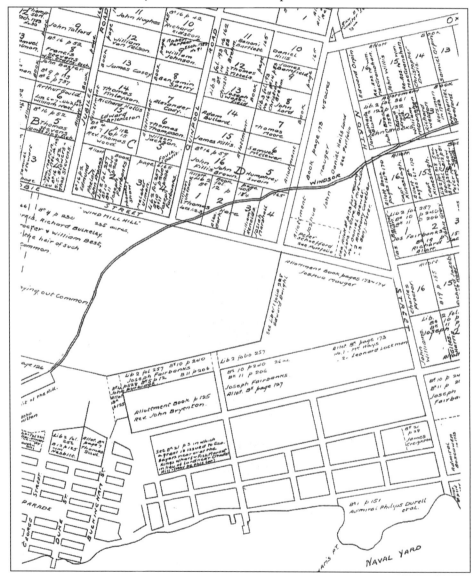

H. Jackson's Map of Original Land Owners, 1945

plans. The assault, though successful, took longer than expected, so many of the regiments and warships had to return to Halifax before setting off the following spring for the assault, also successful, on Quebec. When Haligonians received news of the fall of Quebec, they celebrated wildly for days.

In 1759, Richard Short was purser aboard HMS *Prince of Orange*, part of Wolfe's force awaiting departure for Quebec. While in Halifax, Short, a skilled amateur artist, drew six views of the town. In his view from the Dartmouth shore, he depicts the harbour in preparation for the Quebec campaign. Near the centre is George Street, leading from Citadel Hill down to the King's Slip. St. Paul's Church, built in 1750, is conspicuous to the left of the street at the south end of the Grand Parade. To the right, where the north slope of Citadel Hill descends, Short depicts the north end of town and the leading edge of the old north suburbs. In the north suburbs, there are buildings along the shoreline, while much of the hillside is partially cleared land. Farther north, beyond Short's view, lay the new Royal Naval Dockyard, which began operating that same year. In 1759, the obvious function of colonial Halifax was to serve the military interests of the Crown.

Halifax on the Eve of the American Revolution

Joseph Frederick Wallet Des Barres was a lieutenant in the British 60th Regiment of Foot who ended up in Halifax as part of the military force planning to capture Louisbourg. Des Barres became a trained surveyor. After cessation of war with France in 1763, the British Admiralty recognized the importance of conducting accurate surveys of the shoreline along the east coast of North America, including Nova Scotia. For this huge job, the Admiralty commissioned Des Barres, who worked on the job for ten years. Beginning in 1777, he published his survey maps in *Atlantic Neptune*, an impressive geographical atlas.

RICHARD SHORT'S DRAWING OF HALIFAX FROM THE DARTMOUTH SHORE 1759

Des Barres' published map of Halifax shows the harbour and a variety of topographical features, including relief, drainage, streets, and buildings. It also shows the defences of Halifax before they expanded under threat of the American War of Independence. Gottingen, Brunswick, and Upper Water streets run north from the conspicuous downtown street grid, with Lockman (later Barrington) Street, just west of Water Street, incomplete. The streets are dotted with buildings, notably along the shoreline and uphill from the Naval Dockyard. Within or near the north suburbs there are several commercial wharves: Gerrish's, Mauger's, Hardwell's, Bourne's, Proctor's, and Barnet's. To the north is the Naval Store Keeper's Wharf and farther north, beyond the Dockyard, Mauger's Distillery, an early Halifax landmark. A quarter century after its founding, Halifax had begun to expand.

JOSEPH DES BARRES' MAP OF HALIFAX, EARLY 1770S

Chapter 2

Arrival of Foreign Protestants

REMNANTS OF DUTCH TOWN, 1934

Origin of Dutch Town

During their first months in Halifax, Governor Cornwallis and other colonial officials grew dissatisfied with settlers who were uncooperative and refused to help construct the town defences. They decided to augment British settlers with more industrious Protestant settlers from other countries, so-called "foreign Protestants." In British North America, this practice was then widespread. Private entrepreneurs recruited settlers and

DUTCH COTTAGE, 1952

arranged for ships to transport them as servants indentured to land owners or, as in Nova Scotia, to government, which used their labour for public works.

Between 1749 and 1752, some 2,500 foreign Protestants came to Halifax in this way, almost doubling the size of the town. Twenty-seven families arrived with Cornwallis, while almost all the rest arrived later in special ships. Two thirds of the settlers came from Germany, while the balance came from Switzerland and eastern France. This group included many extended families, with children, parents, and grandparents all seeking a better life. The majority of foreign Protestants settled in the north suburbs, where they were so conspicuous that, following Anglicization, the area became known as Dutch (*Deutsche*) Town.

In 1753, the government relocated most of these settlers to Lunenburg, but a few remained behind, and a few more moved back to build modest wooden cottages on streets named after German families and locations, such as Lockman, Brunswick, and Gottingen. The name Dutch Town stuck with the old north suburbs for decades, and some of the original Dutch cottages survived for almost 200 years.

Two images help evoke how Dutch Town once looked. In 1934, a Dutch cottage stood on the northwest corner of Brunswick Street and Maitland Terrace. Its distinguishing feature was a gambrel-shaped roof (so named because it resembled the shape of a horse's hind leg) modified by a later brick addition to the rear. In 1878, Dr. John Sommers lived in the cottage, when its civic address was 2 Brunswick Street. In 1952, another Dutch cottage stood at 52 Cornwallis Street, on the south side about 80 feet (24.4 metres) east of Gottingen. In the eighteenth century, many such cottages lined unpaved, sometimes grass-grown, Dutch Town lanes. Both Dutch cottages are now gone, the cottage on Brunswick Street demolished in 1954 to make room for a Superline Oils service station.

Digging a Dutch Cottage

Archaeologists can help historians understand the urban past. In fact, they can go beyond historians by uncovering physical remains of buildings and artifacts otherwise known only through pictures and words. In 1986, to demonstrate the usefulness of archaeology, anthropologist Paul Erickson (the author) and a team of investigators from Saint Mary's University excavated a site on the southwest corner of Barrington and Cornwallis streets in former Dutch Town. In 1787, this site was occupied by the cottage of the grandmother of Samuel Sellon, a shipwright who worked at the Naval Dockyard. The cottage burned in that year, leaving behind a tell-tale buried layer of charcoal and artifacts.

The cottage was typical of those once prevalent in this part of the North End, including the two on Brunswick and Cornwallis streets that survived until the

ARCHAEOLOGISTS AT WORK, 1986

1950s. In the 1986 image, the team has excavated the southeast corner of the cottage, revealing its stone foundation and collapsed chimney of fire-cracked stones and bricks. Amidst the rubble, surrounded by charcoal, were shards of storage jars and other ceramics, nails, gunspalls (used to create the spark that fired muskets), pipe bowls and stems, and a flatiron, all dating from the period surrounding 1787. Investigator Dawn Erickson is stooping over in excavation, while Katie Cottreau-Robins takes careful notes and author Paul Erickson explains the excavation to his visiting daughter. Across Barrington Street, not too far south of its intersection with Cornwallis, stands the home of Edith Cormier, the last house demolished on a city block later chosen as the site of a new wastewater treatment plant.

The Little Dutch Church

In 1756, the German settlers who had not relocated to Lunenburg banded together to create their own place of worship. They moved a barn to the northeast corner of Brunswick and Gerrish streets, where surveyor Charles Morris had set aside space for a church and graveyard, and fitted it with twelve rows of pews. In 1760, they expanded the church, originally only 29 feet (8.8 metres) long, and added a bell steeple topped by a chanticleer weathervane, inspiring the nickname Chicken-Cock

SCHOOL AT THE LITTLE DUTCH CHURCH, C.1870

INTERIOR OF THE LITTLE DUTCH CHURCH, 1933

Church. Here, huddled inside and barely protected from harsh weather, worshippers sang hymns and recited prayers in what was, and still is, the first Lutheran church in North America. In 1761, the Little Dutch Church was consecrated as the Church of St. George. In 1800, construction began on larger St. George's Church, the famous Round Church, nearby. Once the Round Church was completed, the Little Dutch Church became affiliated with the Anglican Parish of St. George.

During the nineteenth century, St. George's operated schools for the poor in the Little Dutch Church. The image from around 1870 shows schoolchildren assembled outside, their teacher standing in the doorway. Behind the stone wall is the church graveyard, sheltering many marked and unmarked burials of former Dutch Town residents. The image from 1933 shows the humble interior of the Little Dutch Church, with pews, stove, organ, and altar. Standing near the altar is Rector H. W. Cunningham. Members of the congregation donated many of the visible furnishings and fixtures, including the wooden wainscoting donated by Otto Schwartz. Today the interior and exterior of the church remain much the same, having survived the Halifax Explosion, neighbourhood change, and the wrecking ball of urban renewal. A municipal treasure, the Little Dutch Church, after St. Paul's Church, is the second oldest building in Halifax, an island of continuity surrounded by almost an ocean of change.

A Startling Discovery Beneath the Little Dutch Church

In 1995, the Little Dutch Church was suffering the wear and tear of almost 240 years, so community members began to raise money for necessary repairs. Former German Chancellor Helmut Kohl, while attending the G7 Summit of Western Nations in Halifax, was scheduled to visit the church and make a financial donation. In advance of Kohl's visit, inspectors entered the crawl space underneath the church to assess its structural integrity. There, they were surprised to find three dilapidated brick crypts with human skeletal remains. Repairing the church would require replacing its foundation and adding floor supports, thereby jeopardizing the remains. To investigate and temporarily remove them before repairs, St. George's Church commissioned a team of archaeologists led by Laird Niven and Paul Williams.

The archaeologists worked for several weeks during the summers of 1996 and 1998. In 1996, they carefully documented and removed the crypt burials, later identified at Saint Mary's University under the auspices of anthropologist Paul Erickson (the author). As it turned out, there were historical references to the burials, which, as confirmed by forensic investigation, were the remains of elderly congregationalists Otto Schwartz, his wife Anna Schwartz, and, probably, the Reverend Bernard Houseal. At the time of their deaths, between 1785 and 1799, Halifax cemeteries were crowded and unpleasant places, where people hung laundry, grazed cattle, and dumped waste, and where bodies were surreptitiously dug

EXCAVATING A MASS GRAVE, 1996

up. Christians who could afford it preferred to be buried beneath churches, where their remains would be more secure and respected. There are crypt burials in Halifax not only under the Little Dutch Church but also under St. George's Round Church and St. Paul's Church.

While exploring the ground around the crypts, the archaeologists made a startling discovery—human skeletons stacked side by side and on top of one another in what appeared to be a shallow mass burial trench. They removed the skeletons for safekeeping but were unable to estimate the extent of the trench until 1998, when renewed investigations revealed that it spanned much of the length of the west side of the crawl space, probably containing more skeletons. Anthropological analysis revealed that, unlike the elderly individuals buried in the crypts, the individuals buried in the trench had died relatively young. They were buried without coffins or possessions, wrapped only in burial shrouds. Who were they?

Between 1750 and 1752, foreign Protestants came to Halifax on 11 ships, many of them crowded and unsanitary. The mortality rate on four 1751 crossings ranged between four percent and twelve percent. All but one of the ships were well-ventilated and resistant to epidemic diseases. The *Ann* was poorly ventilated, and when it arrived in September 1750, after twelve weeks at sea, a large proportion of its passengers were sick or dead. More passengers died in Halifax, and 333 Haligonians died in an ensuing epidemic, probably caused by typhus fever (carried by lice). The archaeological investigators inferred from a variety of sources, including burial records, medical histories, and the skeletons themselves, that at least some of these victims of the *Ann* were buried in the mass grave. Six years later, the Little Dutch Church was placed above them.

In the image from 1996, archaeology team member Brent Huber is brushing away dirt that covered one of the skeletons in the trench, exposing for the first time an individual laid to rest 246 years earlier. On August 25, 1998, after having been temporarily removed for protection, all individuals recovered from under the Little Dutch Church were ceremoniously reburied. Their saga is a reminder of the risks and hardships faced by early Halifax pioneers.

AKINS COTTAGE,
1936

Thomas Beamish Akins and His Cottage

As Brunswick Street evolved, gambrel-roofed Dutch cottages were joined by gable-roofed Georgian cottages, such as the one shown here in 1936, built sometime between 1790 and 1821. The cottage, now 2151 Brunswick Street, became home to Thomas Beamish Akins, renowned archivist and bibliophile.

Born in Liverpool, Nova Scotia, Akins grew up in Halifax following the death of his mother when he was young. He was called to the Nova Scotia bar in 1831 and thereafter enjoyed a lucrative law practice, which, with an inheritance, allowed him to retire early and indulge his passion for studying British North American history. In 1839, he wrote a history of early Halifax, which he revised many times, with the last and best-known version published posthumously in 1895. In 1857, Akins became the first Nova Scotia Commissioner of Public Records—in effect, the first Nova Scotian Provincial Archivist—an office he maintained until his death. He collected and catalogued enormous numbers of documents, many of them from other countries. Akins was also a shrewd private collector of books, amassing a library of some 4,000 volumes, now housed at Nova Scotia Archives and Records Management.

When Akins moved to Brunswick Street, the area was no longer just Dutch Town, but many vestiges of old Dutch Town remained, and Akins described them in his written history. He spent much time at home writing, receiving visitors graciously while formally attired in starched collars and broadcloth ties. His portrait, probably dating from the 1870s, captures his description as "old school." In the 1980s, Akins Cottage underwent restoration, and the area to the north, razed earlier in urban renewal, became home to a cluster of new townhouses called Akins Court. Together, the new and old houses convey an air of gentility that belies unflattering stereotypes of this part of the North End.

A North End Success Story

William Schwartz was a true Dutch settler—from Holland—who fled the throes of the French Revolution to Halifax. In 1841, his enterprising son, William Henry Schwartz, began roasting and milling coffee by hand in a shed behind his home on Brunswick Street, launching what was to become the oldest coffee and spice business in Canada. William Henry's equally enterprising son, William E. Schwartz, expanded the business into spices, using only pure spices, not compounds. To convince consumers of the high quality of his products, Schwartz travelled around Nova Scotia, in winter by horse and sleigh and in summer by bicycle, riding the Beeston Humber model, believed to be the first model with pneumatic tires in Canada. His arrival in small towns was highly anticipated, with townsfolk rushing to the road to greet him as he pedalled by and waved.

As it prospered, the Schwartz business outgrew its original location and moved to a larger building stretching from 204 Upper Water Street to 335 Barrington

SCHWARTZ'S, 1914

Street, shown, from the Barrington side, in 1914 (the bicycle is probably William E. Schwartz's trademark model). In 1916, this building burned, and the business again moved, by 1926 ending up in a plant at 826 Barrington Street. The business kept growing, so in 1935 it acquired more space on Cornwallis Street and in 1941 expanded its Barrington Street plant to the south. By this time, the business was incorporated as W. H. Schwartz and Sons and had passed to the fourth and fifth generation of the Schwartz family in Canada. The business remained on Barrington Street until the 1960s, when the city took over the land for urban renewal and Schwartz's relocated to Lakeside Industrial Park.

By the time it left the North End, W. H. Schwartz and Sons was manufacturing—besides spices—mustard, peanut butter, and a variety of other foodstuffs sold in Quebec, Ontario, and thirty countries abroad. No longer did the pleasant aroma of spices waft over the North End, but North Enders had the compensation of knowing that their part of the city had nurtured a major international business success.

BARRINGTON (LOCKMAN) STREET, 1908

The Evolution of Barrington Street

In the North End today, the main harbourside thoroughfare is Barrington Street, running from the South End through downtown all the way to the northern tip of Halifax peninsula. Barrington has not always been one continuous street. For more than a century, it ended at the old north suburbs, where only a footpath connected it to Lockman Street, then running from Cornwallis Street to North. Lockman Street, named after Leonard Lockman, a prominent Dutch Town pioneer, ran parallel to Upper Water Street, the main route to and from downtown and the south end of the dockyard. After 1838, Campbell Road ran from the north end of the Dockyard around the peninsula to the isthmus. All these streets were discontinuous, interrupting the easy flow of traffic.

In 1854, the Nova Scotia Railway completed a line along Bedford Basin ending in a station at the foot of Richmond Street, two miles (three kilometres) north of downtown. Without a continuous thoroughfare, all passenger and freight traffic between downtown and the station had to divert onto Upper Water Street, then bustling with commerce. Later, the Intercolonial Railway extended the line to North Street, where it built a much larger passenger station. In 1871, predicting that the new station would cause traffic bottlenecks, the town connected

Barrington and Lockman streets and then connected them to Campbell Road, creating a continuous thoroughfare.

Early Halifax streets were unpaved, later cobbled with stones and smoothed over with asphalt and concrete. The photograph shows Lockman (Barrington) Street in 1908 after paving. In the foreground, Gerrish Street intersects, and in the background, on the left, the King Edward Hotel at North Street rises above other buildings. Obviously, the old north suburbs had come a long way since Dutch Town.

Chapter 3

The Naval Dockyard

HIS MAJESTY'S DOCKYARD, 1786

Origin of the Dockyard

In the beginning, there were no plans for a naval dockyard to provision and repair ships at Halifax. The British Royal Navy soon realized, however, especially while preparing the campaigns against Louisbourg and Quebec, that it needed just such a facility. In 1758, the navy bought from Joseph Gorham two acres of land in Dutch Town at Gorham's Point, and the following year governor Charles Lawrence contributed seven adjacent acres to the north. On February 7, 1759, an order-in-council formally established the Royal Naval Dockyard.

Navigator Captain James Cook supervised construction of the first Dockyard buildings, and by the mid-1780s, following the American War of Independence, the installations were busily engaged. In 1786, Prince William, son of King George III, paid the first royal visit to Halifax, commanding the frigate *Pegasus*, which anchored offshore. From the *Pegasus*, an artist sketched the town and surrounding area, including the dockyard.

In the *Pegasus* sketch, a masted vessel anchors alongside the careening wharf, the first dockyard facility, where a series of ropes and tackles, called a capstan, could roll a vessel on its side for repairs. While a vessel was being careened, or "heaved over," the officers and crew stayed in the long, multi-windowed building adjacent to the careening wharf, the capstan house. South of the careening wharf, at the far end of the dockyard, stood the commissioner's house, partially blocked in this view by the long, gable-roofed storehouse. Other important facilities in the dockyard were the sail loft, smithy, mast house, and mast pond, where timbers soaked in salt water to remove sap.

The dockyard had expanded several acres north of its original boundary, beyond North Street, which ran to the foot of a fortified hill, Observatory Hill, location of Mauger's Distillery. The southern end of the dockyard began at the foot of Gerrish Street, marked by the Little Dutch Church. Halfway between Gerrish and North streets ran Artz Street, then called Naval Yard Lane, which ended at the main dockyard gate through a perimeter stone wall. Protecting the dockyard were a series of blockhouses along Brunswick Street, and on Observatory Hill, Fort Coote stood watch with three twenty-four-pound cannons. With the dockyard strung out along the water, most of the rest of the North End remained sparsely settled, subdivided by primitive fences and roads.

An Artist Views the Dockyard

After the American War of Independence, renewed conflict between Britain and France accompanied the French Revolution and the rise to power of Napoleon Bonaparte. Once again, Halifax became strategically important and prospered. Attracted by prosperity, English landscape artist George Parkyns travelled to Halifax and engraved four images of the town. Parkyns was drawn to the rural North End, which he idealized in two engravings published in 1801.

Parkyns's view from Albro Cove, Dartmouth, shows the dockyard expanded north of Observatory Hill to new grounds for a naval hospital. Observatory Hill remains (it was later levelled), and the careening wharf and capstan house are conspicuous. The view from nearby Needham Hill, with Fort Needham redoubt on the right, shows major structures in the Dockyard south of North Street. The capstan house, one building with two long ells, resembles a large square, with its fourth side comprising the separate sail loft. The commissioner's house commands

GEORGE PARKYNS'S VIEW FROM DARTMOUTH, 1801

GEORGE PARKYNS'S VIEW FROM FORT NEEDHAM, 1801

a clear view of the harbour, and, to its west, is a new row of dockyard residences just inside the main gate. Since the visit of Prince William fifteen years earlier, much of the North End landscape remained unchanged. It was still unsettled, although less idyllic than depicted by Parkyns. In reality, this was the heyday of privateers, armed merchants who attacked enemy ships, and of press gangs, stronghandlers who rounded up involuntary naval recruits.

The *Shannon* and *Chesapeake* Affair

The War of 1812 dramatically revived activity in the dockyard, which reached its nineteenth-century peak with 104 ships and 1,600 men. The highlight of the war in Halifax was the *Shannon* and *Chesapeake* affair.

In August 1812, the British frigate *Guerriere* encountered the American frigate *Constitution*. A battle ensued, with the surprising result that the *Guerriere* suffered many casualties, was nearly destroyed, and surrendered. A similar fate befell other British frigates, shaking the confidence of the British Royal Navy. In Halifax, Captain Phillip Bowes Vere Broke of HMS *Shannon* vowed to avenge the loss of the *Guerriere*. Unable to locate the *Constitution*, he set his sights on the frigate

SHANNON MONUMENT, c.1882

Chesapeake. Broke challenged Captain James Lawrence to a battle, which the *Chesapeake* lost, along with the life of Lawrence, whose last words—"Don't give up the ship"—became famous.

On June 6, 1813, to great fanfare, the *Shannon* brought the *Chesapeake* into Halifax harbour, with Lawrence's body on deck draped with an American flag. Onlooker Tom Haliburton described the scene graphically.

> The coils and folds of rope were steeped in gore as if in a slaughterhouse. She [the *Chesapeake*] was a fir-built ship and her splinters had wounded nearly as many as the *Shannon*'s shot. Pieces of skin and pendant hair were adhering to the sides of the ship, and in one place I noticed fingers protruding as if thrust through the outer wall of the frigate; while several sailors, to whom liquor had evidently been handed through the ports by visitors in boats, were lying asleep on the bloody floor as if they had fallen in action and expired where they lay.[1]

Captain Broke and many of his crew were wounded, along with many of the crew of the *Chesapeake*, all of whom were treated at the naval hospital. Five crew members of the *Shannon* died and were buried in the nearby naval cemetery. In 1868, the navy restored their original headstone and placed it on a monument, shown in the photograph from around 1882. Almost a hundred years later, in 1966, the Royal Canadian Navy erected another monument to the crew of the *Chesapeake*. Today, these monuments, and the entire naval cemetery, occupy a hill west of north Barrington Street, unnoticed each day by thousands of motorists driving by.

Admiralty House

Despite the importance of the Royal Navy in Halifax, for sixty years the navy lacked a suitable local residence for its admiral. Pressure for a residence mounted, and in 1814 construction began on a Georgian-style mansion east of Gottingen Street overlooking the harbour and naval hospital yard. The mansion was built of ironstone, metamorphosed slate quarried from the west side of the Northwest Arm. Admiralty House took nearly five years to complete and ended up costing more than £4,500.

In 1819, with British global naval superiority established, the navy moved its North American headquarters from Halifax to Bermuda. As a result, Admirality House was used mainly in the summer, when the fleet returned to town. Altogether, thirty-six admirals lived in the house, the last of them Sir Day Hort Bosanquet. The house was the scene of elaborate formal balls and parties, such as the garden party shown in the 1898 photograph. Even grander was an 1848 ball staged by the Earl of Dundonald, attended by 600 guests.

ADMIRALTY HOUSE, 1890s

ADMIRALTY HOUSE GARDEN PARTY, 1898

ADMIRALTY HOUSE GROUNDS, 1890S

Because it was prestigious, Admiralty House attracted prominent Haligonians to north Gottingen Street, where they built their own mansions. One of these mansions was called Clairmont. An 1890s photograph looking north from the rooftop of Clairmont provides a vista of Admiralty House and surrounding grounds. Northward, in the background, loom Wellington Barracks for the military and the Acadia Sugar Refinery belching smoke. By this time, Admiralty House had become an oasis of gentility buffering gracious older estates from the newer industrial suburb of Richmond.

In 1904, thirty-seven years after Canadian Confederation, the British Royal Navy decided to close the Halifax Dockyard, transferring it to Canada officially on January 1, 1907. In 1905, the Navy auctioned off the luxurious furnishings of Admiralty House, and for a while the building stood unused. The 1917 Halifax Explosion damaged the building, and, after repairs, it was used by the Massachusetts-Halifax Relief Committee. In 1925, the Canadian Navy converted it into an officers's mess, serving up to 600 meals a day. In 1954, the mess moved, and the navy converted the building into the Maritime Command Library, now the Maritime Command Museum. Like many naval facilities in Halifax, the Maritime Command Museum is obscured from easy view behind a high ironstone wall. Visitors, however, can easily see that the building looks much the same as it has for close to 200 years.

A City Within a City

In 1878, the Province of Nova Scotia began publishing a series of city atlases to help fire insurance firms, showing building locations, dimensions, uses, and construction materials. The first city atlas of Halifax was prepared under the supervision of civil engineer H. W. Hopkins. One section of Hopkins's atlas covered the dockyard.

In Halifax, the period between the War of 1812 and the First World War was largely peaceful, so the configuration of the dockyard in 1878 was much the same as it had been in its earlier heyday. The buildings and wharves in the old dockyard

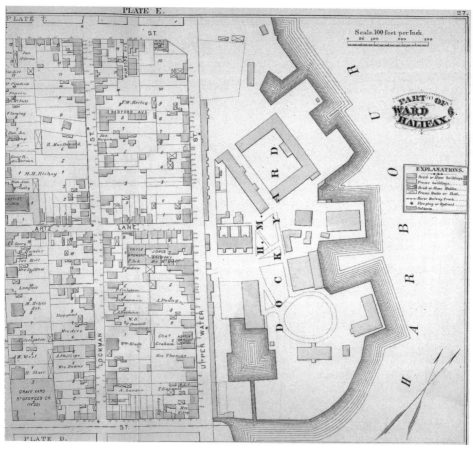

CITY ATLAS OF HALIFAX, 1878
(ABOVE AND OPPOSITE)

south of North Street occupied a space much larger than any adjacent city block. The newer section of the dockyard north of North Street was the victualling and hospital yard, with more buildings inside and along walls. Bordering the dockyard on the west were Lockman Street and Campbell Road, recently linked with Barrington Street. Intruding on the dockyard was the new Intercolonial Railway and North Street station. Even larger than the victualling and hospital yard was the space occupied by Admiralty House, the naval cemetery, and Wellington military barracks. The naval presence in the North End was, and is, a virtual city within a city.

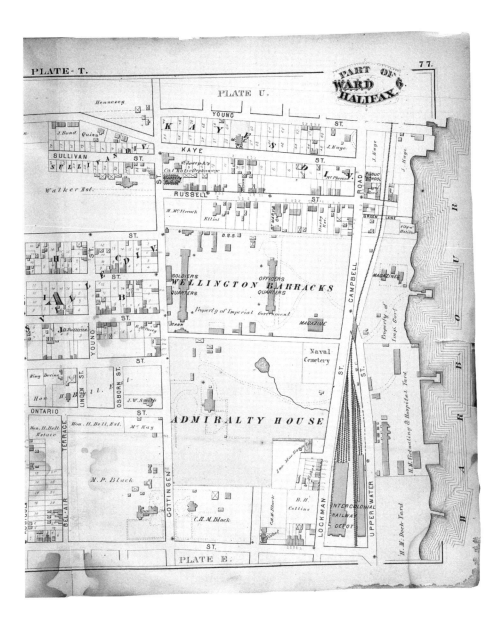

Some Dockyard Buildings

As a city within a city, the old dockyard was elaborate and picturesque. Shown in these photographs is a small sample of buildings, outbuildings, and wharves. The 1870 photograph features the careening wharf, capstan house, and sail loft. The capstan house was an original dockyard installation. In 1760, the navy added two parallel ells, creating the U-shaped building conspicuous in early views. The ells were used to store sails, cables, and other bulky equipment. In 1769, the navy built the sail loft parallel to the capstan house and careening wharf, creating a nearly square building complex. Tied up at the wharf is the naval vessel *Pyramus*, used during medical emergencies as a hospital and quarantine ship. In 1866, the *Pyramus* quarantined the crew of HMS *England* when it threatened Halifax with cholera. At the end of the Age of Sail, the capstan house and sail loft underwent changes, becoming stores, until the navy demolished them during the Second World War.

The photograph from around 1883 shows the south end of the sail loft with a cupola clock. The clock was hand-tooled in London and ran continuously from 1772 until the 1917 Halifax Explosion, after which the navy repaired it and then, when the navy demolished the sail loft, relocated it to the Dockyard fire hall. When the navy demolished the fire hall, it relocated the clock to downtown Halifax, where it is displayed near the Halifax-Dartmouth ferry terminal.

The photograph from around 1882 shows the dockyard commissioner's house, a spacious Georgian residence well situated on Gorham's Point. In 1800, this was the winter residence of the Duke of Kent, who put its ballroom to proper use. When the Royal Navy moved its North American headquarters to Bermuda, the house became an officers' barracks. When the navy transferred the dockyard to Canada, the house stood vacant for several years before burning to the ground in 1909. The cause of the fire is still a mystery.

CAREENING WHARF, CAPSTAN HOUSE, AND SAIL LOFT, 1870

SAIL LOFT, C.1883

COMMISSIONER'S HOUSE, C.1882

Naval Hospital and Victualling Yard

The naval hospital and victualling yard was the newer part of the dockyard, north of North Street, annexed beginning in 1783. The yard began with a hospital, dead house (morgue), "lunatic cells," wharf, and ancillary buildings, including a guard house. In 1809, the navy installed a gate through the stone wall along Upper Water Street. This became the hospital gate, or north gate, contrasted with the older south gate at the foot of Artz Street.

In 1819, fire destroyed the hospital, and there was no permanent replacement for the next forty-four years, although some hospital functions took place in nearby residences. In 1861, four naval vessels brought yellow fever into Halifax, causing alarm and adding pressure for a new hospital. Construction began in 1863 at the location of the old hospital, resulting in the building photographed around 1883. The smaller building along the stone wall is probably the morgue. As in so many contemporary photographs of the North End, in the background the Acadia Sugar Refinery belches smoke. The hospital is also visible in the contemporary photograph of the open hospital gate.

When the British Navy left Halifax, the hospital closed, and in 1910 the building became the Royal Naval College of Canada. The Halifax Explosion damaged the building, and the college closed in 1922, after which it became the Royal Canadian Naval Barracks. In 1916, the navy removed the old hospital gate and

NAVAL HOSPITAL, C.1883

Hospital Gate, c.1883

Victualling Yard Residences, 1926

adjoining wall to make way for a new entrance to the Halifax Shipyards.

The three residences photographed in 1926 date back to 1815, when they occupied the northwest corner of old Fort Coote on land absorbed by the victualling yard. These were the residences that housed temporary hospital functions. Later they became the residences of the secretary clerk, assistant storekeeper, and officer in charge of the works department. They are still in use today, their rooflines and chimneys identifiable from Barrington Street among the many more modern buildings that surround them.

Economic Spin-Off

The dockyard was an economic engine for the North End, spinning off business for local suppliers of labour, materials, food, and, of course, alcoholic drink. Especially profitable were businesses along Upper Water Street between downtown and Gerrish Street, the main route to the south end of the dockyard. This stretch of Upper Water Street also bustled with commerce from wharves, including, in the nineteenth century, the wharves of Samuel Cunard. The west side of the street was a string of tradesmen's shops, confectioneries, eateries, boarding houses, and small

ALLAN HOUSE ON UPPER WATER STREET, 1890s

hotels, such as the Allan House, 282–284 Upper Water, photographed in the 1890s. In the photograph, British sailors pose in front of the house along with, at the far right, proprietor T. D. MacCray. The sailors were probably purchasing supplies for the Dockyard about one block to the north.

The Dockyard in Motion

Photographs of buildings alone cannot effectively convey an image of the intense human activity in the dockyard, both routinely and in times of war. Two photographs show major activities in years leading up to the transfer of the Dockyard from Britain to Canada. The setting is the victualling yard, with the Acadia Sugar Refinery in the background and, in the 1900 photograph, the naval hospital above the roofline on the left.

The dockyard opened in the Age of Sail, but in the late nineteenth century, that age gave way to a new age of iron and steam. In 1869, the first iron-clad ship arrived at the dockyard, and in 1881 the navy demolished old Fort Coote, levelled

COALING HMS *ARIADNE*, C.1898

EMBARKING SS *MILWAUKEE*, 1900

Observatory Hill, and added coaling to its victualling operations. In 1889, north of the victualling yard at the foot of Young Street, contractor S. M. Brookfield built the Halifax Graving Dock to repair the iron-clads, helping launch the phase of North End heavy industry. The 1898 photograph shows the coaling of HMS *Ariadne* underway.

It was almost a hundred years after creation of the Royal Canadian Navy before Canada sent volunteers to help Britain fight a war, the South African Boer War, begun in 1899. Canada sent two volunteer contingents, the first of which departed from Quebec. Because infantry were slow to respond to the Boer's hit-and-run tactics, as the war progressed, there was need for more mounted men. The Second Canadian Contingent of Artillery and Mounted Rifles departed from Halifax in February 1900. Hundreds of Haligonians turned out to watch the troops embark SS *Milwaukee*, shown in the photograph. When the troops returned victorious, even more Haligonians turned out to welcome them home. In the dockyard, the Boer War was a brief rehearsal for the First World War—the Great War—fourteen years later.

Chapter 4

The Military Garrison

NEEDHAM HILL FROM HALIFAX HARBOUR, 1786

Fort Needham

The job of the British military in Halifax was to protect the town and, after 1759, the Naval dockyard. The dockyard began operating during hostilities with France, which ended in 1763 after the capture of Louisbourg and Quebec, thereby establishing British dominance in colonial North America. For a while, the fortifications around Halifax declined, only to be rehabilitated during the American War of

Independence. As a colony that did not rebel, Nova Scotia was vulnerable to potential American attack. Especially vulnerable was the dockyard, which, like the town, could be reached by troops crossing the peninsular isthmus or landing at the Northwest Arm. As Loyalists began arriving in town, they helped spread rumors that General George Washington might order or even lead an attack on the colony. In November, 1776, agitator Jonathan Eddy and a group of disenchanted Acadians and Mi'kmaq attacked Fort Cumberland near the Nova Scotia isthmus. The attack was repulsed, but Haligonians were extremely alarmed.

At the time, the Commanding Royal Engineer in Halifax was William Spry. When trouble began, he hurriedly developed a plan to defend the town, where years of rain and frost had taken their toll on temporary fortifications thrown up during earlier hostilities. The dockyard was located too far north of Halifax to be protected by Fort George on Citadel Hill. To protect it, and Fort George, Spry expropriated several properties in the north end of the peninsula. On properties close to the dockyard he built perimeter bastions and blockhouses, including Fort Coote. On the largest property he built Fort Needham.

Fort Needham was located on the former scenic North Farm of the governor of Nova Scotia, eighty acres (32.3 hectares) bounded today by the harbour, Young Street, Duffus Street, and Novalea Drive. In 1761, the Crown sold the southern half of the Farm to Lambert Folkers, a German settler, and in 1772, Folkers's daughter resold it to James Pedley, an ordnance yard employee. Pedley built a farmhouse at the southwest corner of his property, near what is now the intersection of Novalea Drive and Young Street. In 1776, Spry expropriated eight and three quarter acres (3.5 hectares) north of Pedley's house, where work on Fort Needham got underway in June. The 1786 view of Needham Hill, then called Pedley's Hill, comes from the logbook of HMS *Pegasus*. It shows the hill cleared for fortification, strategically located overlooking the dockyard hospital yard.

The original Fort Needham was a pentagonal earthen redoubt, first called Pedley's Hill redoubt, measuring 900 feet (274.3 metres) around the perimeter and located on the western crest of the hill, oriented toward the peninsular isthmus. It was rimmed with a raised protective berm and ditch surmounted on the east by a wooden bridge. Inside were two barracks for fifty men. Two twenty-four-pound cannons pointed south, supporting fire from the north face of Citadel Hill, and two more twenty-four-pounders pointed west toward a hill near the isthmus, McAlpine's Hill (Strawberry Hill). If McAlpine's hill had been captured, it might have threatened the dockyard.

About 400 feet (122 metres) north of the redoubt, at the border of the governor's North Farm, Needham Hill began a steep descent, which, at the time, the enemy might have ascended secretly. There Spry began work on an octagonal wooden blockhouse. The blockhouse was never completed, possibly because of the successful defense of Fort Cumberland. The 1778 plans of Fort Needham redoubt were drawn by William Spry. The namesake of the Fort is unknown but probably was either Captain Francis Jack Needham or Lieutenant John Needham, descendants of the House of Kilmorey who served in Nova Scotia.

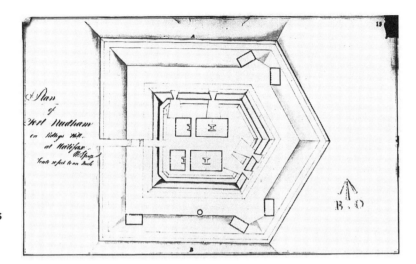

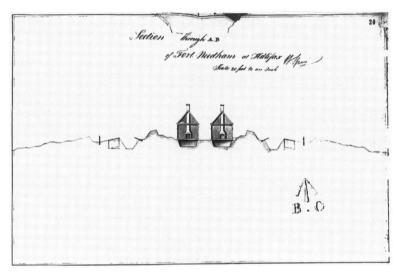

Around 1780, army officer Edward Hicks painted a vista from Fort Needham during the American War of Independence. The vista affords a clear view of the town, Citadel Hill, the dockyard, and Fort Coote. The fenced road between the town and Fort Needham is Gottingen Street, leading to the governor's North Farm past James Pedley's farmhouse, whose roof and chimney are visible above the stone wall. The farmhouse remained at this location for more than a century. In the 1850s, it was the home of Joseph Jennings, Halifax mayor and merchant. Jennings's daughter Amelia Clotilda Jennings wrote poetry describing the stately chestnut and linden trees on the property, so the house became known as Linden Hall. In 1890, Saul Mosher purchased Linden Hall and demolished it, replacing it with a wood-frame house that was one of the few in the area to survive the Halifax Explosion. Abandoned, the ditch and berm depicted by Hicks caught the eye of artist George Parkyns when he viewed the dockyard from the same location in 1801.

FORT NEEDHAM ON GUARD, C.1780

Fort Needham Eclipsed

Following defeat in the American War of Independence, Britain ought to have reinforced its fortifications in Halifax, capital of its principal remaining North American colony. Instead, weary and demoralized, it allowed the fortifications to deteriorate. In June 1807, the British frigate *Leopard* intercepted the American warship *Chesapeake* to search for deserters. Several men were forcibly removed, tried in Halifax, and two of them flogged to death on the waterfront. The Americans were incensed, and colonial secretary Lord Castlereagh feared retaliation. He instructed governor John Wentworth to beef up the militia to help soldiers protect Halifax by rebuilding its defenses.

General Maslin Hunter wanted to rebuild Fort Needham as an enlarged redoubt enclosing a Martello-type stone tower. There was insufficient time to execute this plan, so the redoubt was rebuilt along its original lines, with the berm protected by stakes and parapets along its flanks. This time, the blockhouse was completed to accommodate sixty soldiers and mounted with two twelve-pound cannons. Rebuilt Fort Needham stood guard during the War of 1812 and the global threats of Napoleon Bonaparte, but two years after Napoleon's defeat in 1815, it once again lay in ruins. Local residents vandalized and dismantled the blockhouse, which blew down in a windstorm.

As an extended peace in North America continued on, many British politicians wanted to wash their hands of unused and expensive military installations. The Duke of Wellington, head of the ordnance department, was more far-sighted and decided to take advantage of peace by planning for future wars. In 1825, he sent a

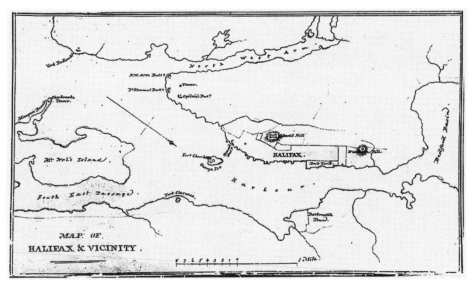

NEEDHAM HILL AND CITADEL HILL, 1825

three-man commission headed by James Carmichael Smyth on a fact-finding tour of Canada. The Commission recommended twenty-one new military installations, including, for Halifax, a masonry fort on Citadel Hill, two towers at the peninsular isthmus, a tower south of the Citadel at Fort Massey, and a tower north of the Citadel at Fort Needham. An 1825 sketch from the commission's report shows how Citadel Hill and Needham Hill were intended to function together in defense of the dockyard.

The Smyth Commission's recommendations were extraordinarily expensive, exceeding the budget of the ordnance department for defending the entire British Empire. The report was mired for years in controversy, and the only recommendation ever approved for Nova Scotia was the masonry fort on Citadel Hill. Work on the new Citadel began in 1828 and required thirty years to complete, costing more than twice its original estimate. Ironically, by the time the Citadel was completed, it had become militarily obsolete, because breech-loading ordnance had replaced smooth-bore cannon, increasing the range of fire ten times. Without further modification, no military installation, including Fort Needham, could effectively protect Halifax from attack by sea or land.

Throughout the nineteenth century, Fort Needham remained largely unchanged. In the 1850s, the British army built impressive new barracks, the Wellington Barracks, on nearby land to the south. Regiments from the barracks used the fort's open spaces for training and recreation, including polo, shown in the photograph from around 1885. After the Halifax garrison passed from Britain to Canada, the Royal Canadian Regiment continued to use the property. In the summer neighbourhood children played cowboys and Indians on the berms of the old redoubt, and in the winter they skated on ice in its ditches. The photograph from the 1920s shows that even after the Halifax Explosion, traces of the redoubt and path to the blockhouse remained etched in the landscape. Meanwhile, south of the redoubt, Saul Mosher's house survived among the trees that gave its predecessor, James Pedley's farmhouse, the name Linden Hall.

PLAYING POLO ON FORT NEEDHAM, C.1885

TRACES OF FORT NEEDHAM REDOUBT, C.1920s

Wellington Barracks

Military barracks have long been located in various places around Halifax. For almost a century, they were constructed of wood, and often they burned. In the 1830s, the navy began planning for permanent masonry barracks on twenty-one acres (8.5 hectares) of land between Fort Needham and Admiralty House. In 1850, it approved plans for two large brick barracks, one for officers and the other for enlisted men, on opposite sides of a spacious parade ground. Winning a bid for

ROYAL CANADIAN REGIMENT AT WELLINGTON BARRACKS, c.1906

DRUMS AND
FIFES OF THE
ROYAL
CANADIAN
REGIMENT
BAND AT
WELLINGTON
BARRACKS
AROUND 1906

£43,271, the firm of Peters, Blaiklock, and Peters started construction the following year, but cost overruns delayed completion until 1860. The completed barracks were surrounded with a high ironstone wall, and in 1863 a bombproof magazine was added. Accommodating 641 military personnel, they were named after the Duke of Wellington, the British soldier who defeated Napoleon at the Battle of Waterloo.

Wellington Barracks were soon occupied by the Royal Canadian Regiment, the oldest permanent regular infantry unit in Canada. Parliament created the regiment in 1883, beginning with three companies in New Brunswick, Quebec, and Ontario. Special battalions served in the Boer War or stayed at the barracks while regular British troops engaged in service. When the British army left Halifax, the Royal Canadian Regiment reorganized to occupy the vacated garrison. It secured headquarters, formed six companies, and maintained a tour of duty for the next forty years. The two photographs from around 1906 shows the regiment drawn up for parade in front of the officers' quarters at Wellington Barracks and also the drums and fifes of the regiment band. The photograph from around 1900 shows the band marching through the barracks gate from Gottingen Street near Almon Street. Clearly, although separated by a wall, the barracks were very close to this North End neighbourhood.

ROYAL CANADIAN REGIMENT BAND AT THE ENTRANCE TO WELLINGTON BARRACKS, C.1900

The Military Complex Near Citadel Hill

The centrepiece of the Halifax garrison was Fort George on Citadel Hill, which, although never used in battle, is now visited annually by of thousands of tourists. Owing to fires and demolitions, these tourists cannot see the succession of military installations that once occupied the north slope of the hill and nearby streets.

Of the five original perimeter forts, Fort Luttrell, with barracks, stood near the northeast corner of Citadel Hill. Around 1759, the army built two additional barracks below Fort Luttrell on the west side of Barrack (Brunswick) Street between Buckingham and Jacob. These were the Red Barracks, two and one half storeys tall and separated by a large parade ground. Designed to accommodate more than a thousand men, the Red Barracks were landmarks on the Halifax skyline for decades, as shown in the 1791 view. They lent their name to Barrack Street, then lined with brothels and bars.

VIEW OF THE RED BARRACKS, 1791

In 1794, Prince Edward, Duke of Kent, became military commander-in-chief at Halifax, a post he retained until 1800. During his stay, he invested large sums of money in fortifications. Under his guidance, the army expanded the glacis, or slope, of Citadel Hill along Cogswell Street and added new North Barracks. These barracks were two parallel blocks, each four and one half storeys, set perpendicular to the Red Barracks, forming a square. In 1806, on the slope above the North Barracks, the former town house of Prince Edward became a military hospital.

In 1847, the army built a garrison chapel on the northwest corner of Cogswell and Brunswick streets. This classic-style wooden building was designed for 724 worshippers, with officers and their families in the galleries and non-commissioned officers and men on the floor. The 1901 photograph shows the chapel with military men attending a memorial service following the death of Queen Victoria.

In 1850, fire destroyed the North and Red barracks, putting pressure on accommodation for soldiers, pressure that was relieved somewhat by completion of the more fire-resistant Wellington Barracks. By 1870, the army had replaced the North

Parade Garrison Chapel Memorial Service for Queen

Norman Studio
8323

GARRISON CHAPEL, 1901

GLACIS AND PAVILION BARRACKS, 1884

GLACIS BARRACKS GUARD ROOM, C.1879

and Red Barracks with the Pavilion Barracks, married soldiers quarters built on the same site but with three rather than four blocks. Many Haligonians continued to refer to the Pavilion Barracks as the North Barracks.

In 1866, the military hospital also burned. Nearby, the army had already begun work on a new block of two and one half storey Glacis Barracks. Following the fire, it added an identical second block on the burned hospital site. By 1870, the army had also built a grand new garrison hospital on the northeast corner of Cogswell and Gottingen streets. The 1884 photograph shows the Pavilion Barracks and Glacis Barracks, with the garrison chapel behind the Glacis Barracks, and, to their left, the garrison hospital. The 1879 photograph shows sentries on duty at the Glacis Barracks guard room.

Farther away from the Citadel was the ordnance yard, located along the water at the foot of Buckingham Street near the original North Battery. To protect passers-by, the yard was walled, and, at its south end, Upper Water Street was diverted toward Hollis. The yard was an eclectic mix of wooden and ironstone storehouses, wharves, and specialized facilities such as the armoury and laboratory. The 1904 photograph shows Companies 98 and 103 of the Royal Garrison Artillery assembled on the coal wharf.

In preparation for its departure from Halifax, the British army renovated old military installations and built several new ones along Cogswell and Brunswick streets. These included a military gymnasium, warrant officer's residence, army

COMPANIES 98 AND 103 OF THE ROYAL GARRISON ARTILLERY AT THE ORDNANCE YARD, 1904

service corps office, supply depot building, and, north of the garrison chapel, a row of twelve brick residences known as the Church-field Barracks, reserved for married men. On January 16, 1906, the imperial government formally turned over the entire Halifax garrison to the Dominion of Canada to be administered by the Department of Militia and Defense. In 1928, fire destroyed the garrison chapel, and it was replaced by Trinity Church. Eventually, as they outlived their perceived usefulness, most of the other military buildings succumbed to the wrecking ball. As a result, hardly anything remains of the tough military face once presented to this part of the North End.

The Halifax Armouries

Before the Canadian Department of Militia and Defence took over the Halifax garrison, it contributed only one building, the Halifax Armouries. In 1894, the department expropriated the city block facing the Halifax Common bounded by North Park Street, Maynard Street, Cunard Street, and Johns Lane. By 1899, it built there a new militia headquarters and "drill shed" to replace overcrowded facilities on Spring Garden Road. Hardly a shed, the new Halifax Armouries was the

CANADIAN MOUNTED RIFLES OUTSIDE THE ARMOURIES, C.1900

THE ARMOURIES IN WARTIME, OCTOBER 30, 1941

best facility of its kind in Canada, an imposing, castle-like structure able to accommodate 8,000 people. Almost all the building materials came from Nova Scotia, including large amounts of sandstone and granite. Crowds hailed the first militiamen as they moved in on the eve of the Boer War. During the war, the armouries housed several militia units, including Troop Three, D Squadron, of the Canadian Mounted Rifles, photographed outside around 1900.

The armouries opened in late Victorian times, when socially prominent Haligonians worked diligently for charitable causes. On June 21, 1899, taking advantage of both space and the lustre of a military connection, one socially prominent group staged at the armouries the largest charity ball Halifax had ever seen. A dazzling affair, it raised money to build a new Infant's Home, where "illegitimate" children of unwed mothers were shielded from poverty and social stigma. Ironically, or appropriately, these children included the offspring of soldiers.

For more than a hundred years, the Halifax Armouries have served Canada in times of peace and war. They were especially busy during the First World War, when they stored relief supplies for victims of the Halifax Explosion, and the Second World War, when military personnel and equipment occupied the common, as seen in the 1941 photograph. Today, with almost all the old garrison buildings gone, the armouries bear important witness to the rich military legacy in Halifax, celebrated annually in the Nova Scotia Tattoo.

Chapter 5

Gradual Expansion North

HALIFAX FROM DARTMOUTH, C.1830

Major North End Roads

The view of Halifax from Dartmouth around 1830 shows that the town
had grown modestly since the War of 1812. The Red Barracks were conspicuous on the slope of Citadel Hill, and to the north, buildings dotted
the shoreline and were scattered uphill. Still, much of the North End
remained open fields and farms that were neither frequently nor heavily
used in peacetime. As the North End gradually expanded, it both created

and extended roads. Most of these roads were parallel or perpendicular, reflecting Charles Morris's original suburban plan. Four major roads, however, were irregular, because their purpose was, and still is, to provide transportation on and off the Halifax peninsula.

The first road off the peninsula was Windsor Street—the road to Windsor—which began west of the Halifax Common at Bell Road and ran northwest toward Bedford Basin. By the time of the American War of Independence, Gottingen Street, which began in Dutch Town, stretched north to Fort Needham and the governor's North Farm. In 1781, lieutenant-governor Sir Andrew Snape Hamond built a farmhouse near the governor's farm at what was then the far end of Gottingen Street (now Novalea Drive). For his convenience, the government built a road westward from the far end to meet Windsor Street at the peninsular isthmus. In honour of his wife Anne, the lieutenant-governor named the new road Lady Hamond (now spelled Hammond) Road.

In 1820, Sir James Kempt became lieutenant-governor of Nova Scotia. Kempt, an army officer turned colonial administrator, had a penchant for road building. Realizing that horse-drawn carts had difficulty ascending the steep hill at the north end of Windsor Street, he constructed an alternate, more level route to and from the isthmus. Kempt Road, as the alternate became known, began at Robie Street just south of Young Street and ran around the foot of the hill to meet Windsor Street and Lady Hammond Road. Kempt envisioned another road around the perimeter of the peninsula from the isthmus to central Halifax. This vision was realized a few years later by lieutenant-governor Sir Colin Campbell, another army officer turned colonial administrator, who understood that good roads would build economic prosperity. Campbell supervised completion of the perimeter road, Campbell Road, as far as the north end of the dockyard, where it promoted the growth of Campbell Town, later called Richmond. Campbell's broader vision was of a road completely circling the Halifax peninsula, through downtown, around

SIR JAMES KEMPT
(c.1765–1854)

SIR COLIN CAMPBELL
(1776–1847)

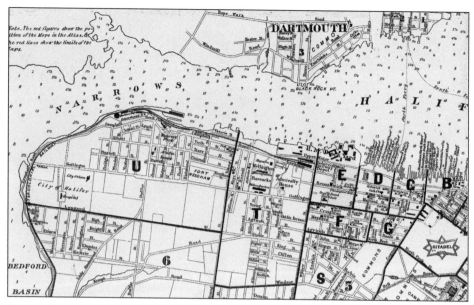

NORTH END ROADS, 1878

Point Pleasant, and along the isthmus back to Bedford Basin. This vision was realized only incompletely when Campbell Road was linked with Lockman and Barrington streets to form a single artery.

The 1878 map from *City Atlas of Halifax* shows Windsor Street, Lady Hammond Road, Kempt Road, and Campbell Road, along with other parallel and perpendicular North End streets. For a long time, these were unpaved country lanes, dotted with inns and coffeehouses for travellers making journeys that were then time-consuming and adventurous.

A Famous Duel

Early in the morning of July 21, 1819, four shots rang out over the governor's North Farm, leaving one man mortally wounded and Halifax in shock. The shots resulted from a duel between William John Bowie and Richard John Uniacke, son of the attorney general. While prosecuting a trial in Supreme Court, the junior Uniacke, an attorney, had implied that Bowie was a smuggler. Bowie was a popular merchant who made money from buying and selling ships. With his business reputation, as well as his honour, at stake, he formally protested. When Uniacke refused to retract his implication, Bowie challenged him to a duel, which Uniacke accepted.

Following protocol, the two men met before dawn at a grove near the governor's North Farm. Assisting them were their "seconds," Edward M'Sweney for Uniacke, and Stephen DeBlois for Bowie. M'Sweney, an experienced army officer, supervised the duel. In the first exchange of shots, neither man met his mark.

According to one account, both Uniacke and Bowie were willing to stop at this point, but M'Sweney urged them on. In the second exchange, Uniacke's bullet passed through Bowie's body. Mortally wounded, he slumped to the ground and was rushed to a nearby farmhouse, where he died.

Many Haligonians attended Bowie's funeral two days later, while flags in Halifax flew at half mast. On July 27, a grand jury issued indictments of murder against Uniacke and M'Sweney. Their trial took place the following day, accompanied, as such sensational trials are today, by considerable notoriety. The senior Richard John Uniacke ushered his son into court and presented him to the judge. By the end of the day, after hearing testimony from witnesses, a jury acquitted both men of the charge. While M'Sweney suffered public criticism, Uniacke went on to become a member of the House of Assembly and serve on the provincial Supreme Court. Observers remarked that Uniacke never psychologically recovered from the experience and remained melancholy for the rest of his life. The unfortunate Uniacke-Bowie encounter was the last, if not the only, fatal duel recorded in Nova Scotia.

Arrival of the Cunards

In the nineteenth century, a major impetus for expansion along Upper Water Street was the arrival of the Cunards. Abraham Cunard settled in Halifax in 1783 and worked as a carpenter for the Royal Engineers. His homestead was a small building at the rear of a lot on the east side of Brunswick Street. By almost all accounts, this homestead was the birthplace of Abraham's son Samuel. Abraham purchased lots along the water downhill from his homestead on the east side of Upper Water Street in order to build warehouses and wharves. In 1812, with Samuel, he founded A. Cunard & Son to buy and sell timber, some of it to the nearby dockyard, and otherwise engage in West Indies trade. Two Cunard waterfront structures became Halifax landmarks. One was Cunard's Wharf, the largest area wharf, and the other was the Cunard ironstone office and warehouse, photographed around 1916.

After Abraham died in 1824, Samuel, already de facto head of the company, changed its name to S. Cunard & Company. Despite financial ups and downs, the company continued to grow by buying and selling ships and contributed significantly to the prosperity of Nova Scotia's golden Age of Sail. In 1838, Samuel won a potentially lucrative contract to launch a transatlantic steamship service carrying mail and passengers between Liverpool and Boston via Halifax. In May 1840, the first Cunard experimental steamer, the *Unicorn*, arrived in Halifax to a cheering crowd of 3,000 spectators. Two months later, the first regularly scheduled steamer, the *Britannia*, arrived to an equally enthusiastic reception. Haligonians expected so much economic spinoff from the new Cunard enterprise that they raised £8,000 to build a hotel for the anticipated influx of visitors. For a while, there was some city-wide spinoff, with excitement and glamour centred on Cunard's Wharf. Soon, however, it became apparent that Halifax was only a stopover on the way to Boston, and by 1876, Cunard steamships discontinued regular calls.

When the Cunards first arrived on Upper Water Street, the street was lined with houses and businesses that had sprung up en route to the dockyard. When Samuel launched his steamship service, new businesses appeared, including hostelries such as the European Hotel, photographed in 1934. In 1842, Charles Dickens visited the hotel en route to Boston on board the *Britannia*. In his *American Notes*, he recalled his visit.

SIR SAMUEL CUNARD (1787–1865)

I suppose this Halifax would have appeared an Elysium, although it had been a curiosity of ugly dulness [*sic*]. But I carried away with me a most pleasant impression of the town and its inhabitants, and have preserved it to this hour. Nor was it without regret that I came home, without having found an opportunity of returning thither, and once more shaking hands with the friends I made that day.[2]

CUNARD FAMILY HOME AT 257 BRUNSWICK STREET, C.1870

S. CUNARD & COMPANY OFFICE AND WAREHOUSE ON UPPER WATER STREET, C.1916

In the late 1800s, railways, already established in the North End, pushed farther south to new Deep Water terminals between North Street and Proctor's Lane. The dominion government of Prime Minister Wilfrid Laurier nurtured the development of Deep Water with lots of money. In 1907, it bought the Cunard waterfront property for $187,000, setting in motion the demolition of Cunard's Wharf, office, and warehouse to make way for the modern Pier 2. The office and warehouse was so well constructed that its demolition in 1917 required heavy dynamite. Workers salvaged a cache of old coins and artifacts dating back to an era of maritime commerce that the demolition symbolically brought to a close.

Back in the early 1800s, Samuel Cunard had built a family home at 257 Brunswick Street, photographed around 1870 as the second house north of Proctor's Lane. In the 1960s, the Halifax Development Company acquired the building and demolished it to make room for a parking lot for the Trade Mart of Scotia Square. The site is now occupied by Cunard Court apartments. Admirers of Samuel Cunard hope that someday Halifax will erect a suitable monument to his memory.

A Block of Time

The city block bounded by Upper Water Street, Barrington Street, Cornwallis Street, and Proctor's Lane was one of the most vital blocks in North End Halifax. The map from *City Atlas of Halifax* shows that in 1878 it was occupied by more than sixty buildings, including those of S. Cunard & Company and J. J. Scriven & Sons bakery. In subsequent decades, the block changed character as it survived the Halifax Explosion, the Great Depression, and the Second World War. What it did not survive was planned post-war urban renewal, which by the 1980s had led to the demolition of all but one building and returned the block to where it began— urban wilderness.

In the late 1990s, as part of its strategy to combat harbour pollution, the Halifax Regional Municipality began planning for a wastewater treatment plant on the block. In 2001, it hired Cultural Resource Management, a group of consulting archaeologists headed by Bruce Stewart, to conduct an archaeological reconnaissance of the site, and in 2002 it hired the same company to conduct excavations. The 2002 photograph shows archaeological excavations in progress. The goal was to salvage artifacts and document underground features threatened with destruction. Identifying the artifacts and features required knowing the history of the block, which researchers Paul Erickson (the author) and Dawn Erickson compiled. Their research revealed that over the course of its more than 250-year history, the block was home to thousands of people from diverse walks of life, countless home-based occupations, and commercial enterprises: Allan House, Al-Molky Dry Goods, Arnolds Bakery, Atlantic Sheet Metal Works, Atlas Locker Rentals, Barrington Shoe Repair, Charles Stoneley Grocery, Chicago Café, Chittick and Sons Ice House, The Coffee Shop, Cornwallis Taxi, D. A. Cummings Sheet Metal Works, Dyno-Tec Irving, Empire Café, European Hotel, F. J. Quinn Mineral Waters, F. W. Bedwin Company, Fred's Speed Shop, George's Café, Halifax Judo Academy, Halifax Marine Engineering Company, Halifax Social Assistance Office, Halifax Surf Club, Hobin's Variety Store, Honeywell Controls, Ideal Home Equipment, International Varnish, Jewell Grocery Store, J. J. Scriven and Sons Bakery, Johnson's Bakery, Keefe's Shoe Repair, Mahar's Transfer Express, Metro Turning Point Centre, New Magic Café, Nova Scotia Beverage Company, Pilkington Brothers, Pitney Bowes of Canada, Renault Maritimes, Ring Boxing Club, St. Patrick's Hall, S. Cunard & Company, Steamship House, Sydney Café, T. Hogan & Company Boilermakers, T. P. Calkin Heating Supplies, Thomas O'Malley Grocery, Tom McDonnell's Downtown Garage, Victoria House, Viscount Metal Products, Western Union Telegraph, William Ford Liquors, and William S. Craig Plumbing and Heating. This long list shows in detail what urban archaeologists mean when they say that, even where nothing remains on the surface, something may be lurking under ground.

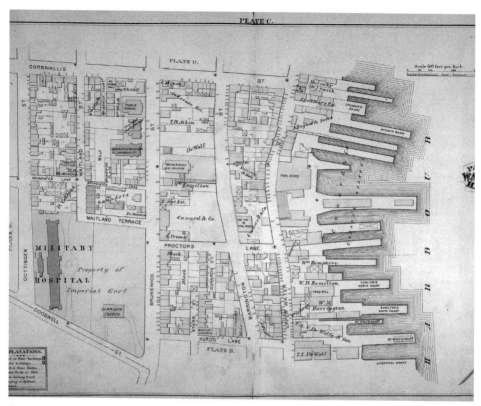

THE BLOCK, 1878

THE BLOCK, 2002

Proud Brunswick Street

Brunswick Street began as a country lane through old Dutch Town, soon linked to Barrack Street at the northeast corner of Citadel Hill. The street is shorter than other parallel North End streets because it becomes a dead-end at the property of Admiralty House and Wellington Barracks. It was the location of a succession of Dutch cottages, Georgian cottages, and Victorian mansions. In the nineteenth century, as Halifax grew, and people with financial means sought refuge from a crowded downtown, Brunswick Street became a residential address of distinction, offering large lots for gardens and a splendid harbour view. Accompanying the upper echelon of Halifax society to Brunswick were dignified places of worship: St. Patrick's Roman Catholic Chapel and Church, Brunswick Street Universalist Church, and Brunswick Street Methodist Church, shown in the streetscape from the 1860s or 1870s.

The most architecturally distinctive church on Brunswick Street was St. George's Round Church. The predecessor of the Round Church was the Little Dutch Church, consecrated to St. George in 1760. As its congregation grew, the Dutch Church became too small, so in 1800 work began on a new St. George's Anglican Church at the northwest corner of Brunswick and Cornwallis. The Duke of Kent, who liked round buildings, supported the new church, which started out simply circular. In the 1820s, a chancel and vestry were added, creating the configuration shown in the 1880s photograph, where a horse-drawn cart is pumping water. St. George's Round Church has always been a Halifax landmark, attended by eminent Haligonians such as one-time neighbour Samuel Cunard. On June 2, 1994, a terrible fire destroyed or severely damaged a large part of the church. A concerted effort by parishioners, community members, and three levels of government raised $4,600,000 to help restore St. George's to its former architectural glory.

Both middle-class tradesmen and upper-class merchants who amassed wealth in West Indies trade found Brunswick Street attractive. One wealthy merchant was John Conrad West, grandson of a German settler whose surname was Wust. The firm of C. West & Son operated three wharves, ten stores, and eight ships, headquartering at West's Wharf adjoining the Naval Dockyard. Five of West's sons carried on the family business and, because the family was close-knit, all built houses on Brunswick Street. Son John Conrad West built the ornate Italianate villa photographed around 1880 when its civic address was 321 Brunswick Street. His brother Augustus W. West lived a short distance away at 385 Brunswick Street, two doors north of the Little Dutch Church. The photograph of the A. W. West family gathered in front of their carriage house around 1890 gives an impression of how upper-class Brunswick Street residents lived in the late Victorian era. Altogether, so much eminence and architectural distinction accumulated on Brunswick Street that today, despite many demolitions, the street is home to almost thirty designated heritage properties.

In the 1950s, Halifax launched an ambitious program of urban renewal, resulting in the demolition of scores of old buildings along the waterfront, downtown,

BRUNSWICK STREETSCAPE, 1860S OR 1870S

and in the north suburbs. As demolitions proceeded, citizens began to protest, and in response Halifax City Council created the Halifax Civic Advisory Committee on the Preservation of Historic Buildings. The job of the committee was to evaluate the condition and historical significance of remaining buildings in order to determine which ones might be preserved. In 1967, under the chairmanship of Louis W. Collins, the committee turned its attention to Brunswick Street, where demolitions were underway. In 1968, it published a survey of buildings remaining on the east side of Brunswick between Cornwallis and Gerrish streets, recommending that the majority of the buildings there be spared.

The Brunswick streetscape, drawn by L. B. Jensen, shows some of the buildings included in the 1968 survey. On the left (north) is the mansion of John Conrad West, and on the right are Saint Patrick's Rectory and Roman Catholic Church. With a little imagination, proud Brunswick Street in its heyday reappears.

Succeeding the Civic Advisory Committee was the Halifax Landmarks Commission, followed by the City Heritage Advisory Committee, created under the auspices of the Provincial Heritage Property Act. The act provides a legal framework for registering heritage properties, maintaining them, and helping protect them from demolition. As a result, public appreciation of built heritage is enhanced. Looking at Brunswick Street today, with so many old buildings gone, heritage advocates can hope that such far-reaching demolition does not recur.

ST. GEORGE'S ROUND CHURCH, 1880s

South Gottingen—The People's Street

Like Brunswick Street, Gottingen Street began in old Dutch Town but, unlike Brunswick, it extended farther north, to Fort Needham and the governor's North Farm. By 1820, there were still very few houses along Gottingen, even close to town, where the street ran alongside Creighton's and Maynard's fields. One house at Gottingen and Gerrish Street was dubbed the North Pole.

In ensuing decades, Gottingen steadily developed along its north and south ends. In the south, it became a lively community of homes, shops, and civic institutions that took on a life all its own. The 1901 streetscape shows the west side of

RESIDENCE OF JOHN CONRAD WEST, C.1880

A. W. WEST FAMILY GATHERING, C.1890

BRUNSWICK STREETSCAPE, 1968

Gottingen north of Cornwallis Street. At the corner is George A. Cook and Company, pork and provision dealers; next door is Owen P. Hill, tailor; and farther north, with flags flying, is McPherson and Freeman dry goods store—"The People's Store."

As Gottingen approached North Street, its character began to change. The homes became more stately, and dominating the east side of the street was the distinguished Institution for the Deaf and Dumb. The institution began in 1858 with funds from benefactors, student fees, and legislative grants. In 1861, it served forty-four pupils, thirty boys and fourteen girls, who learned reading, writing, arithmetic, and Bible-based Christianity. The photograph of the building dates from around 1890. The photograph of students and staff from around 1883 includes, probably in front, the family of principal H. F. Woodbridge. In 1896, the building was demolished to make way for a larger brick building, which in turn was demolished in 1962 to make way for Uniacke Square.

North Gottingen Street

North of North Street, Admiralty House acted as a magnet for prestigious estates that came to occupy Gottingen Street and farmland to the west. Outstanding were the estates of Bloomfield, Belle Aire, Bellevue, and Clairmont.

Bloomfield was located west of Gottingen Street and reached by a long narrow road, now Bloomfield Street. Built sometime before 1838, it was the retreat of the Honourable Hugh Bell, mayor of Halifax, who moved there in the 1840s. The

GOTTINGEN STREETSCAPE, 1901

INSTITUTION FOR THE DEAF AND DUMB, C.1890

STUDENTS AND STAFF OF THE INSTITUTION FOR THE DEAF AND DUMB, C.1883

estate was architecturally Georgian, with a distinctive semi-circular dormer window. Bell operated a soap factory at the rear of the property, which sat in a field of blooming daisies, inspiring the estate's name. After his death, his heirs maintained the estate for a while but then, in the 1880s, subdivided it for building lots. They created a new residential neighbourhood on streets such as Ontario and Fuller Terrace, where the Bloomfield house still stands.

South of Bloomfield was Belle Aire, estate of John Northrup, built in 1815 on a five-acre lot with a long driveway from North Street. In 1870, the Roman Catholic Church acquired the estate and for several years operated it as Saint Mary's College. When the church sold unwanted portions, it provided for building subdivisions separated by Belle Aire Terrace and a section of Agricola Street. A subsequent owner moved the house south to align it with new houses on North Street. In 1913, a telephone company acquired the house, which was so badly damaged in the Halifax Explosion of 1917 that it was razed and replaced by the red brick building now spanning the old driveway.

More ostentatious than these two estates were Bellevue and Clairmont, a pair of mansions on the northwest and northeast corners of Gottingen and North streets. Bellevue, with ornamental trees, flower-beds, and fountains, was built in 1821 as the home of Martin P. Black. Martin's brother Charles H. M. Black lived across the street in Clairmont, a large estate extending from Gottingen Street to

Lorne Terrace, with a rooftop affording a panoramic view. After Black's death, Clairmont passed through a succession of owners to become the officers' quarters and mess of Wellington Barracks and later the Home for Aged Men. The 1936 photograph of this elegant property shows how it rivaled the finest estates built later in the South End. The last owner, CFB Halifax, demolished it. Bellevue had been subdivided at about the same time as Bloomfield, when part of its carriage drive became Black Street. The building survived for many years until it was razed for Northwood Manor.

The hubbub of Wellington Barracks, the pressure for residential land, and the passing of an era of refined wealth all contributed to the progressive subdivision and development of the area bounded by Gottingen, Robie, North, and Young streets. With the addition of large properties owned by the Bilby, Macara, and Sullivan families, the process was completed by around 1900. The result was a respectable and middle class part of the North End, different from both the diversified old north suburbs to the south and the burgeoning industrial suburb of Richmond farther north.

BLOOMFIELD HOUSE, 1928

CLAIRMONT HOUSE, 1936

Agricola

Many of the large farms in the far North End were owned by German settlers, one of them Philip Folmar. In 1784, Folmar built a retreat among beautiful willow trees on a tract of land along the road to Windsor, north of what became Almon Street. Later, this tract, Willow Park, was acquired by Scottish settler John Young. Young had moved to Halifax in 1814, when the town was still prospering from the War of 1812. After the war, prosperity declined, and he became alarmed that so much agricultural land was devoted to raising food for the British army and navy. Young published a series of influential anonymous letters in the newspaper *Acadian Recorder* advising Nova Scotians how to become more agriculturally self-sufficient. He signed the letters "Agricola."

In 1819, to put his agricultural ideas into action, Young bought Willow Park and operated it as an experimental farm, putting at least 70 of its 80 acres (28.3 of 32.4 hectares) into cultivation. After his death in 1837, his family put the farm up

JOHN YOUNG (1773–1837)

for sale, and in the 1870s, Bennett Hornsby, an ex-American Confederate Army colonel, bought it as a real estate investment. After 1896, the Halifax street railway put Willow Park within easy commuting distance of downtown, and Hornsby's investment paid off. Soon former Willow Park was a leading edge of Halifax's residential West End. One of its original buildings, Waverley Cottage, remained on the corner of Windsor and Almon streets until 1947. The memory of John Young survives in the name of two North End streets, Agricola and Young. Young Avenue in the South End is named after his son William, who switched from farming to a career in law.

Robie Street

One of the largest North End farms belonged to John Longard, a hardware merchant who could afford to live on Brunswick Street but who wanted a retreat outside the city. Around 1812, Longard built his retreat on top of a hill north of Lady Hammond Road. The access road was Longard Road, later the far north end of Robie Street. Longard's dwelling was simple, but among its outbuildings was an unusual windmill that operated with horizontally rotating canvas sails. A subsequent owner moved the dwelling southwest to align it with Robie Street, where it remained until at least the 1930s. The photograph shows the house in 1936, looking bleak, like a small part of the Great Depression. The vacant land behind it stretches onto a bluff overlooking Bedford Basin with, in the distance, Rockhead Prison, the Infectious Disease Hospital, and, below, Africville.

LONGARD HOMESTEAD, 1936

Chapter 6

Impact of Railways

RICHMOND STATION, C.1868

The Nova Scotia Railway

In Halifax, railways arrived first in the North End, where they served as infrastructure for industry and triggered population growth and neighbourhood change. By the mid 1800s, Nova Scotia sought a railway to unify the colony and transport food from outlying fertile areas into Halifax. There was debate, however, about whether the railway should be privately or publicly funded. Thomas Haliburton and Joseph Howe helped persuade the

RICHMOND, C.1890

government to operate the railway, leading in 1854 to incorporation of the publicly owned Nova Scotia Railway. On June 13, 1854, sod was turned for the new railway along Campbell Road at the governor's North Farm. Attending the ceremony were lieutenant-governor Sir John Harvey, members of the Railway Board, and about a hundred of the thousand labourers required for construction. The projected route was around the northern tip of Halifax peninsula and along Bedford Basin to Windsor Junction, where it forked toward Windsor and Truro.

The Halifax terminus of the railway was a passenger and freight depot near the foot of Duffus Street in Richmond. Its construction sparked a rise in property values and a flurry of new construction. The Richmond depot, photographed around 1868, was an unadorned wooden building with attached wings, or sheds, penetrated by a single track. In the early days, without telegraph service, trains had to wait longer for clearance to pass, so, like depots elsewhere, the Richmond depot provided its customers a saloon, where they could buy bread, tea, and beer. Some passengers got "liquored up" before boarding the train, while others quenched their thirst at Windsor Junction, where the train stopped to discharge passengers and freight and take on fresh water and fuel wood. Because little time was required for loading and unloading horse-drawn carts, service could be surprisingly rapid. In 1855, a ride from Richmond to Four Mile House, an inn located about one mile beyond the peninsular isthmus, took only five to seven minutes. Trains departed daily at 3 PM and 5 PM and returned a half an hour later, charging a round trip fare of one York shilling. The promise of the railway seemed almost endless, and both users and owners enthusiastically geared up for the future.

What the near future brought was heavy industry, transforming Richmond into an industrial suburb of Halifax. The photograph from around 1890 depicts the area as gritty, much like one of its stereotypes today. The area would have been even grittier if it had become the repair and maintenance headquarters of the succeeding Intercolonial Railway. That facility instead went to Moncton, because, some

Haligonians griped, the Dominion government wanted to punish Halifax for being the seat of so much opposition to Confederation.

The Intercolonial Railway

After Canadian Confederation in 1867, the Nova Scotia Railway became part of the Intercolonial Railway, which the new Dominion government wanted to link Halifax with the Great Lakes. A priority for the Intercolonial was a new Halifax depot that would be larger, grander, and closer to town than the rambling wooden depot two miles north at Richmond. The government considered numerous potential sites, including the North Common, but was unable to convince the Imperial government to grant passage through the dockyard. Therefore, it settled on a site on the north side of North Street between the dockyard and Admiralty House grounds. The new station was for passengers only, with freight still handled at Richmond.

In 1875, the Department of Public Works called for tenders for the new North Street station. Henry Peters won the competition and built the grandest station Canada had ever seen. The imposing main building, resting on a granite base and clad in the finest pressed brick, rose two storeys with a third-storey mansard roof surmounted by a tall central tower. Passengers approached the building from North Street and entered the main waiting room finished with paneled wainscoting and varnished pitch-pine floors. There were four ticket windows, including one for telegraphs. To the east was the ladies' waiting room, with a separate ticket office, plush seats, and marble mantle with mirror. The second storey housed offices for railway officials and a bal-

NORTH STREET STATION AND KING EDWARD HOTEL, C.1903

cony on the north side overlooking the passenger shed. The central tower showcased a modern electric clock with multiple dials. The passenger shed was 400 feet (122 metres) long, with eight massive doors and eleven dormer windows on each side and twenty-four iron trusses supporting a glass-covered roof. On August 8, 1877, prime minister Alexander Mackenzie and friends rode into the station on the first passenger train, and the following day the station officially opened for business.

Although the North Street station spunoff local commerce, for many years it lacked a companion hotel. In 1902, William Wilson met this need by becoming the first proprietor of the King Edward Hotel, conveniently located opposite the station at Barrington (Lockman) Street and North. This handsome, five-storey wooden building, photographed around 1903, boasted seventy-five rooms for as many as two hundred guests paying $2 per night and up. The King Edward Hotel and North Street station were the equivalent of the Hotel Nova Scotian (now the Westin Nova Scotian) and Canadian National Railway station built later in the South End. On December 29, 1911, a fire ravaged the King Edward, causing $100,000 worth of damage. The hotel survived the 1917 Halifax Explosion and during the Second World War was occupied by the Canadian navy, which later demolished it. The North Street station met a worse fate. The explosion destroyed it, collapsing its glass roof, lifting and twisting rails, tossing railcars into the harbour, and killing sixty employees.

City Railways

The incursion of provincial and national railways into Halifax led to the creation of intra-city railways. For more than a decade after the Richmond depot opened, only horse-drawn cabs provided connecting service, charging exorbitant fares as high as fifty cents. Then in 1866, to great relief, William O'Brien opened the horse-drawn Halifax City Railway. The tracks ran from the depot south along Campbell Road to Upper Water Street, then through downtown, and eventually as far as Inglis Street. At first, weekday cars operated every fifteen minutes from 6 AM until 10 PM, charging reasonable fares of seven cents for adults and three cents for children. Ten years later, construction of the new North Street station required tearing up part of Upper Water Street, eliminating O'Brien's tracks. Railway officials asked O'Brien to relocate his tracks to Lockman Street, but he refused and instead ceased operations. For the next ten years transportation to and from the station reverted to horse-drawn cabs.

In 1886, the Halifax Street Railway, an American company, resumed horse-drawn rail service, expanding routes and adding extra horses to pull cars up steep hills. The railway ran into financial difficulties and in 1890 was taken over by the newly incorporated Nova Scotia Power Company. The power company intended to electrify the rail system but it too ran into financial difficulties and in 1895 was succeeded by the Halifax Electric Tramway Company. The tramway company installed poles and overhead wires and inaugurated electric car service on February 12, 1896. Three months later, on May 31, 1896, the horse-drawn cars ceased oper-

HALIFAX STREET RAILWAY HORSE BARN AT CAMPBELL ROAD AND HANOVER STREET, 1894

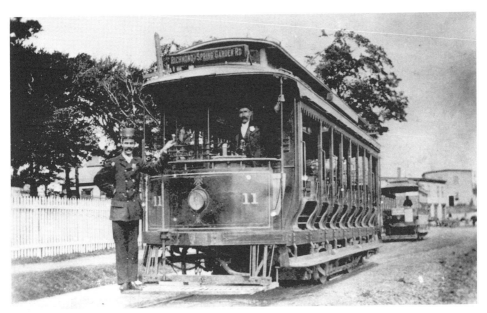

HALIFAX ELECTRIC TRAMCAR 11 AT BARRINGTON AND ROOME STREETS, 1897

ation on their last remaining route, along Barrington (Lockman) Street between Cornwallis and Duffus.

The 1894 photograph shows employees of the Halifax Street Railway in front of the railway horse barns at Barrington and Hanover streets. On the far left stands superintendent James Adams, who bought the horses when the railway went out of business two years later. The 1897 photograph shows tramcar 11 of the new Halifax Electric Tramway Company idling at the corner of Barrington and Roome streets, conducted by Gill Ring. In addition to the original line along Barrington Street and an extension along Spring Garden Road, tramcar service expanded along Cunard, Gottingen, Agricola, and Almon streets to Willow Park. The Halifax Explosion damaged many tramcars as well as overhead poles and wires. In 1920, to upgrade its cars, the company introduced new Birney models, which operated until 1949, when they were superseded by electric trolleys and still later by diesel buses.

Halifax Harbour Bridges

All bridges across Halifax harbour have had an impact on the North End. The first bridge was an Intercolonial Railway bridge spanning the narrows at Richmond. Built in 1885, it was a wooden trestle with deep supports and a manually-operated swing section in the middle. Before pollution, Halifax harbour sometimes froze over in winter, so to deflect blocks of ice leaving Bedford Basin, the bridge was contoured with a concavity facing north. In 1891, fierce winds blew up the harbour and smashed the bridge to pieces. The following year it was rebuilt, and in 1893 it was again destroyed by high tides. Another bridge was not completed until 1955, when the Angus L. Macdonald bridge opened at North Street, followed in the 1970s by the A. Murray MacKay bridge at the narrows.

A legend predicts that the Angus L. Macdonald bridge will also suffer destruction. As the legend goes, in early Halifax a young Mi'kmaw male loved a Mi'kmaw maiden, but the maiden instead loved a white settler, or pale-face. The settler came to the maiden's wigwam and asked her to accompany him to the beach, where they kissed and set out together in his boat. The native youth observed the two lovers and went after them in his canoe. Pulling up next to them, he drew a hatchet to kill the settler but by mistake killed the maiden, who sank beneath the waves while the settler escaped to shore. The youth then threw his hatchet into the water, raised his hand to heaven, and swore:

> Three times a bridge o'er these waves shall rise,
> Built by the pale face, so strong and wise,
> Three times shall fall like a dying breath,
> In storm, in silence, and last in death.[3]

Whether the legend predicted the future is open to interpretation. The first Halifax harbour bridge fell in a storm, and the second fell in high tides that may have been silent. The legendary fate of the third bridge, the Angus L. Macdonald bridge, is best judged uncertain.

FIRST HARBOUR BRIDGE, C.1890

The Railways Push South

The Intercolonial Railway station at North Street was a beachhead for further railway expansion south. The station itself was located on the west side of Upper Water Street, but a narrow line on the east side allowed tracks to continue by, or more accurately through, the dockyard to Gerrish Street, where they fanned out to meet a new Deep Water terminal. Deep Water, completed by 1880, could accommodate vessels larger than those at the shallower waters of Richmond. In the late 1800s and early 1900s, thousands of Canadian immigrants passed through this facility. Construction of Deep Water spurred expansion and repair of commercial wharves along Upper Water Street. In anticipation of new business, S. Cunard & Company started to buy and sell coal, storing it in large sheds north of its office and warehouse and on Cunard property along Proctor's Lane. In 1882, the Dominion government spent $100,000 to build a huge wooden grain elevator on the east side of Upper Water Street north of Cornwallis Street. In 1895, the elevator and adjacent parts of the Deep Water terminal ignited in a spectacular fire, spewing chunks of burning wood throughout the neighbourhood. Repaired, the damaged terminal survived, but the grain elevator was replaced four years later by a newer elevator on the west side of Upper Water. The view north from around 1900 is from the roof of this second elevator. Much of the old dockyard is discernable on Gorham's Point, although a section has been displaced by railway tracks. The west side of Upper Water Street is a nearly continuous row of buildings stretching to North Street and beyond to Richmond.

LOOKING NORTH ALONG UPPER WATER STREET, C.1900

After Britain turned over the dockyard to Canada, the government of prime minister Wilfred Laurier embarked on an ambitious and costly program of railway and port expansion. It bought the old waterfront wharves and buildings of Samuel Cunard and demolished them to make way for Pier 2. Railway spurs linked the pier to points north along a freight shed that ran almost the entire length of Upper Water Street between Proctor's Lane and Cornwallis Street. The shed blocked visual and actual access to the harbour, transforming the character of the neighbourhood. Before railways, the waterfront around Cunard's wharf was old-fashioned and colourful. After railways, it became more anonymously industrial. Still, the waterfront remained busy. During the First World War, almost all Canadian soldiers leaving for and returning from Europe used Pier 2, a number surpassing 280,000.

Why did the railways not expand farther south to downtown Halifax? There were two reasons: downtown property was prohibitively expensive, and the whole route through the North End was judged unsightly. With huge amounts of money invested in Deep Water and Pier 2, city council made an extravagant decision. It authorized a new railway cut through bedrock all the way from the peninsular isthmus through the West and South ends to a new terminal near Point Pleasant Park. Work was already underway when the North Street station was wrecked in the Halifax Explosion. After the First World War, the new railway complex that developed between Point Pleasant Park and Terminal Road—with depot, hotel, piers, tracks, and grain elevator—was essentially a clone of the old complex in the North End.

Chapter 7

Promise of Industry

RICHMOND BEFORE INDUSTRY, 1860S

Richmond Industrializes

For a while, the railways failed to promote heavy industry in Richmond, because Canadian Confederation damaged reciprocal trade with the United States and sent the local economy into a tailspin. In the 1860s, Richmond remained pre-industrial, as it appears from the distance in the photograph of a regatta at the Royal Nova Scotia Yacht Club (later the Lorne Boat Club). Within a few years, however, the

NOVA SCOTIA SUGAR REFINERY, C.1880

HALIFAX GRAVING DOCK UNDER CONSTRUCTION, C.1888

Dominion government adopted what it called the National Policy, a set of protective national tariffs that subsidized Canadian industry. In 1879, when this policy came into effect, industrialization took off. By the end of the nineteenth century, Richmond was a burgeoning industrial suburb of Halifax, boasting several installations whose stature was world-class.

Richmond industries located along the waterfront and inland on flat land. Two major waterfront industries were the Nova Scotia Sugar Refinery, located between Hanover and Young streets, and the Halifax Graving Dock, located just south of the refinery between Young Street and the dockyard. The refinery was incorporated in 1880, privately capitalized with $300,000, and publicly subsidized with an exemption from taxes and a supply of free water. Refining sugar from its raw crystallized state was an expensive and complicated operation conducted in a huge facility constructed by S. M. Brookfield. The photograph of the refinery from around 1880 shows its several components, including a ten-storey filter house, the tallest structure in Canada east of Montreal, and an eight-storey sugar house, where the raw sugar, imported from Brazil, was boiled. At its peak, the refinery operated around the clock with 120 employees each day producing 500 barrels of refined sugar, conveniently transferred onto Intercolonial Railway cars for shipment.

The Halifax Graving Dock was highly touted by the city of Halifax and the British Admiral, who wanted a facility capable of graving, or repairing, large steel-hulled ships. An annual government subsidy of $30,000 aided the formation, in England, of the Halifax Graving Dock Company, capitalized with $1 million. Construction of the dock, photographed around 1888, was challenging and expensive, requiring blasting out bedrock. The walls and floor required 5,000 tons of concrete, and the floor was covered with heavy pitch pine. The dock closed with a massive floating gate, and it emptied with powerful engines able to evacuate 40,000 gallons of water per minute.

The Admiral designed the dock large enough to accommodate HMS *Inflexible*, the widest warship in the world. The finished length of the dock was 568 feet (173.2 metres). Along the North Atlantic, Halifax was behind only New York and Boston in the number of steamships using its port. The new dock had the advantage of accommodating the largest of these ships without having to remove their guns or cargo. On September 21, 1889, the Halifax Graving Dock opened officially with a ceremonious appearance of HMS *Canada*. In 1918, after the Halifax Explosion, the Halifax Shipyards took over operations at the same site.

Besides the sugar refinery and graving dock, other major waterfront industries were Hillis and Sons Foundry, manufacturer of stoves and furnaces, and the Gunn and Company milling plant, importer of large shipments of grain from Richmond, Virginia—probably lending the Richmond district its name.

Additional industries chose to locate away from the waterfront on an expanse of flat land bounded by Robie Street (Longard Road), Kempt Road and Windsor Street. The largest industry there was the Nova Scotia Cotton Company, a massive facility occupying 30 acres (12.1 hectares) at the corner of Robie and Young Street. Capitalized with $300,000, it owned 400 looms operated by 300 employees, most

HALIFAX GRAVING DOCK, 1889

of them young women, a work force that would be considered economically signifi-cant in Halifax even today. To encourage the cotton company, the city allowed the Intercolonial Railway to build a branch line along Kempt Road from the factory to the isthmus and around Bedford Basin to Richmond wharves. This branch, and a later secondary branch, converted the area into a virtual industrial park, eventually comprising, at the corner of Young and Kempt, the Nova Scotia Paint Works, at the corner of Windsor and North Street, the Nova Scotia Car Works, and, at the corner of Young and Windsor, the repair shops of the Intercolonial Railway. All these inland and waterfront industries flanked a residential area that was home to blue-collar workers who toiled in the factories and helped them generate profit.

The cotton company was destroyed in the Halifax Explosion, which sent tons of heavy machinery crashing through floors, crushing employees. In 1918, Piercey's Building Supplies acquired the property and began manufacturing materials badly needed for reconstruction. Even before the explosion, Richmond industries had declined, suffering from a shift in population and political power from eastern to central Canada. In central Canada, an abundant supply of coal and steel and a nat-ural transportation waterway along the Great Lakes and St. Lawrence River made

CANADIAN INDUSTRIES LIMITED FERTILIZER PLANT, 1941

industry more attractive. When the Intercolonial Railway was completed between Halifax and Montreal, central Canadians bought Halifax industries and consolidated them with their own interests. The Nova Scotia Sugar Refinery became the Acadia Sugar Refinery, and the Nova Scotia Cotton Company became Dominion Textiles. The fate of the refinery exemplifies the fate of industrialized Halifax: raw sugar was unloaded at Halifax harbour, transferred onto railcars, shipped to Montreal, refined and packaged, and then shipped back to Halifax for sale.

Although the promise of industry in Halifax was short-lived, North Enders can be proud of the enterprise and skill they contributed to industrial growth. After the explosion, industry persevered in the North End, taking advantage of its railways, harbour, work force, and industrial tradition. Typical was Canadian Industries Limited (CIL), which operated a fertilizer manufacturing plant at Pier 9 near the foot of Duffus Street. Another legacy of North End industry is the corridor of businesses along Young Street around the imprint of the old Intercolonial Railway branch line.

DOMINION EXHIBITION BUILDING, 1906

INDIAN CAMPS AT THE EXHIBITION, 1905

Exhibiting Nova Scotian Industry

Nova Scotia was the first British colony to stage an exhibition of its agriculture and industry. The exhibition took place in 1854 on the grounds of Province House and was repeated in 1868. Hoping to repeat the exhibition again every ten years, the province established a permanent exhibition grounds at Tower Road and Summer Street, a site now occupied by All Saints Cathedral. In the 1890s, with the exhibition growing, the province searched for more spacious grounds, eventually deciding on 30 acres (12.1 hectares) west of the Dominion Textiles factory in the North End. This land was largely open, level, and serviced by street and industrial railways. The provincial and dominion governments agreed that the new exhibition would be an annual affair.

In 1897, work began on a complex of buildings bordered by Young, Almon, and Windsor streets. On September 28, the new Exhibition Grounds, costing $100,000, opened to great fanfare. Besides the main building, with its trademark central dome, the grounds featured buildings for machinery, transportation, agriculture, and dairying. Six horse barns, two cattle barns, and a sheep and swine building housed and fed thousands of animals. Behind the main building, a grandstand for 4,000 spectators overlooked a half-mile (0.8 kilometre) racing track. Near the track were animal show rings, an amusement stage, and two lagoons for high diving and aquatic sports. This was the most impressive exhibition grounds in Canada.

For the 1897 exhibition, expected to attract 60,000 visitors, admission was twenty-five cents for adults and fifteen cents for children. The first daily program featured a band concert, military tournament, trapeze show, and fireworks, along with performances by parachutists, bicycle and unicycle riders, and serpentine and fire dancers. In 1912, the first airplane flights over Halifax took place from the Exhibition Grounds, a milestone marred by one horrifying crash. In the years leading up to the Halifax Explosion, so exciting was the annual exhibition that children in Richmond climbed Needham Hill to try to catch a glimpse of the goings-on. A paean to industrial progress, the exhibition was suitably located in Halifax's North End.

FORMER HOME OF SAUL MOSHER AT THE CORNER OF YOUNG AND GOTTINGEN STREETS, 1936

The Richmond Community

Richmond was not all smoke, steel, and industrial commotion. It was also a community. The community began as Campbell Town along Campbell Road, then expanded up Needham Hill with the appearance of the Nova Scotia Railway. In 1854, realizing the possibility of local development, the Nova Scotia government relinquished its hold on the governor's North Farm and subdivided it for private sale. This action led to the creation of an east-west, north-south grid of gravel roads. North from Young Street and parallel to Gottingen Street and Campbell Road ran Needham, Union, Albert (sometimes Starr), and Veith streets. West from Campbell and parallel to Young and Duffus ran Hanover, Richmond, Ross, Kenny, and Roome streets. Among these roads, slated for houses, the government reserved three green spaces: Fort Needham, Mulgrave Park, and Acadia Square.

The land west of Fort Needham between Young Street and Lady Hammond Road had been occupied by farms. Much of it was Merkelsfield, named after the Merkel family, one of the largest farm owners. In 1891, with Richmond expanding, the Halifax Land Company bought Merkelsfield and subdivided it for housing, creating streets such as Merkel, Kane, Hennessey, and Stairs, as well as the

GROVE PRESBYTERIAN CHURCH WITH REVEREND JOHN F. DUNSTON c.1912

KAYE STREET
METHODIST
CHURCH c.1910

ST. MARK'S ANGLICAN CHURCH AND THE ROYAL CANADIAN REGIMENT, C.1909

boulevard that later became north Agricola Street. In both Merkelsfield and Richmond proper, the names of streets reflected local history: Merkel and Veith for early landowners; Needham for a British soldier associated with the Fort; Victoria, Albert, and Hanover for the Royal connection; and Duffus, Kenny, Roome, Stairs, and Starr for prominent citizens and industrialists.

Location of smokestack industries in Richmond branded it working-class, but the community was by no means a slum. Most houses were respectable, if plain, flat-roofed wooden dwellings, distinct from the older row houses and tenements south of North Street. The stereotypical Richmond resident was a hard-working, God-fearing, Irish or Scots immigrant, such as the character Big Alec MacKenzie in Hugh MacLennan's novel *Barometer Rising*. Like all stereotypes, this one is only partially accurate. Several business owners and managers lived among the workers of Richmond. One was George A. McKenzie, manager of the Acadia Sugar Refinery, who lived at 77 Young Street in a handsome house with a mansard roof, built in 1891 by Saul Mosher. As the 1936 photograph shows, this house, which survived the Halifax Explosion, was surrounded by stately trees dating back to the time when Amelia Clotilda Jennings lived on the property and gave it the name Linden Hall.

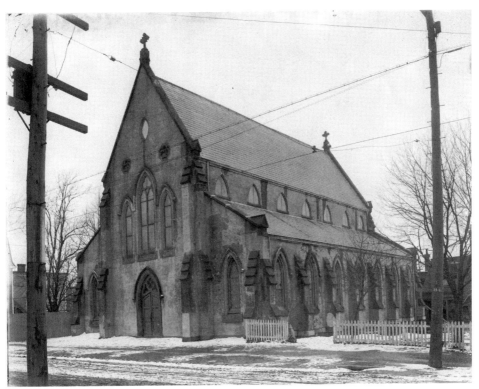

ST. JOSEPH'S ROMAN CATHOLIC CHURCH BEFORE THE HALIFAX EXPLOSION

To communities come churches, and to Richmond came four, all built at around the same time. Two were Grove Presbyterian Church and Kaye Street Methodist Church. Grove Presbyterian, photographed around 1912, was built in 1872 between Duffus and Roome streets. Architecturally similar Kaye Street Methodist Church was built in 1869. The Halifax Explosion destroyed both churches, killing 131 members of Grove Presbyterian alone. After the explosion, the two surviving congregations occupied a temporary tar paper-covered church near the corner of Gottingen and Young streets. They later united into the Kaye-Grove congregation and built a new church on the site of Kaye Street Methodist. When the new church opened in 1920, it bore the name United Memorial Church, representing the first such union in Canada.

St. Mark's Anglican Church was consecrated in 1866 as a chapel for St. George's Round Church. In 1881, at the request of the nearby dockyard, it became a separate parish. Located on the south side of Russell Street abutting the property of Wellington Barracks, the church enjoyed strong military as well as naval connections. Around 1888, it added two side aisles and a new chancel to make room for military and naval attendees. Military bands played at services and open air concerts, as shown in the photograph from around 1909, with neighbourhood children observing the band of the Royal Canadian Regiment. The naval connection also generated a prestigious annual summer garden party held on the grounds of St. Mark's or nearby Admiralty House. Two hundred St. Mark's parishioners died in the Halifax Explosion, which destroyed their church and spared only a melted communion chalice and altar cross. After the explosion, new neighbourhood businesses appeared, notably the Halifax Shipyards, which employed 2,000 people, contributing parishioners. In 1920, the cornerstone was laid for a new St. Mark's church on Gottingen Street, and the following year the first service took place there.

St. Joseph's was the first Roman Catholic Church in the far North End. It was the vision of Father Thomas Vincent Allen, who supervised construction at Gottingen and Russell streets. Before the church was completed in 1867, Father Allen taught Sunday school at the Richmond railway depot. After the church was completed, he lived in a nearby house donated, along with church land, by alderman Daniel Sullivan. The Sisters of Charity soon joined St. Joseph's Parish, operating an orphanage and a school. The parish began with fifty families, a number that by 1916 had risen to 600. The Halifax Explosion destroyed St. Joseph's and killed almost 400 parishioners. In 1920, the church reopened in a basement on the original site, and in 1959 the parish built a new church there. The new church and original church were both architecturally Gothic, providing some continuity in a community that had experienced a horrific disruption.

Chapter 8

The Halifax Explosion

IRA MCNABB'S CLOCK, C.1917

Ground Zero

> It was five minutes after nine,
> As those alive can tell,
> That the beautiful city of Halifax,
> Was given a taste of Hell.[4]

In 1906, the British army and navy withdrew from Halifax, having shaped the history of the city for more than 150 years. Four years later, Canada created its own navy with a single Atlantic ship, HMCS *Niobe*. When the First World War began, the Royal Canadian Navy was woefully unprepared for battle, so the British navy returned to Halifax to help. As usual in wartime Halifax, the population swelled, city services strained, and prices soared. The city became one of the busiest ports in the world, handling 15 million tonnes of cargo annually, up more than 700 percent from pre-war times. The war raged for three years before the United States entered it in 1917, joining Canadians in the common cause of fighting "the Huns." American ships also joined Allied Atlantic convoys assembling in Bedford Basin for the perilous voyage to Europe. With the nearby basin, railways, industry, and naval installations all devoted to wartime activities, nowhere in Halifax was the impact of the war greater than in the North End community of Richmond.

In early December 1917, the French freighter *Mont Blanc*, captained by Aimé Le Medec, left New York for Halifax to join an Atlantic convoy. It was carrying an explosive cargo of 35 tonnes of flammable benzine in barrels lashed to its deck and 2,300 tonnes of picric acid and 200 tonnes of TNT in its holds. Reaching the outskirts of Halifax harbour on December 5, it lay anchor and waited for permission to enter Bedford Basin the next morning under the guidance of harbour pilot Francis Mackey. Meanwhile, in the basin, the Norwegian ship *Imo*, captained by Haakon From, was anxious to get underway for New York to pick up relief supplies for Belgium. Because the *Imo*'s mission was humanitarian, the ship was draped with a protective sign that read "Belgian Relief." A delay in coaling prevented the *Imo* from leaving before submarine nets blocked the harbour for the night, so it too, along with the *Mont Blanc*, awaited safe passage early the following day.

The morning of December 6, 1917, was clear and cold as Richmond residents went about their normal wartime routines. At first, accustomed to a congested harbour, hardly anybody was concerned about the *Mont Blanc* as it proceeded toward the Narrows, a constriction in the water along Richmond at the mouth of Bedford Basin. Following established procedures, the incoming *Mont Blanc* kept to its starboard, or Dartmouth, side of the harbour, so that outgoing ships could pass on its port, or Halifax, side. Captain Le Medec was alarmed to notice the outgoing *Imo* also on the Dartmouth side, on a collision course with his ship.

After an exchange of whistles, Captain Le Medec ordered the *Mont Blanc* to veer toward port. At about the same time, Captain From ordered the *Imo* to veer toward starboard. The *Imo* then reversed its engines, throwing its bow into the bow of the *Mont Blanc*. With its engines still in reverse, the *Imo* disengaged, gnashing the two steel hulls and causing sparks that ignited benzine spilling from ruptured barrels into the holds of the *Mont Blanc*. At about 8:45 AM, the *Mont Blanc* was engulfed in a fierce fire that sent plumes of dark smoke and bright flames skyward.

Following the collision, the *Imo* drifted toward Dartmouth, and the *Mont Blanc* drifted toward wooden Pier 6 at Richmond, threatening to set the pier aflame. Captain Le Medec, deciding that he could not control the fire, and fearing its consequences, ordered his crew to abandon ship. Lowering two lifeboats, they rowed quickly to the Dartmouth shore. In Richmond, unaware of the deadly cargo of munitions, hundreds of people flocked to their windows, rooftops, streets, and the top of Fort Needham to observe the spectacle. A few minutes later, from his grocery store on Campbell Road, Constant Upham alerted the fire department, which dispatched the *Patricia*, its first motorized engine. Firefighter William Wells drove the *Patricia* to Pier 6, where Chief Edward Condon ordered his crew to man the hose and try to save the pier, declaring the *Mont Blanc* itself a lost cause.

Meanwhile, in the harbour, the salvage tug *Stella Maris* headed for the two ships, ending up between them about 150 yards (137.2 metres) from the burning *Mont Blanc*. Both HMS *Highflier*, anchored at mid-channel, and HMCS *Niobe*, tied up at the Dockyard, launched boats to provide assistance. Naval officers pulled alongside the *Stella Maris* and conferred with Captain Horatio Brannan, who told his crew to break out a thick rope and try to tow the *Mont Blanc* out into the harbour. Elsewhere, another courageous man, telegraph operator Vincent Coleman, was dispatching trains at Richmond Station. Train number 10, an overnight express from St. John, New Brunswick, was scheduled to arrive at 9 AM but was running ten minutes late. First leaving the station, then in good conscience returning, Coleman wired the prophetic warning: "Munition ship on fire. Making for Pier 6. Goodbye."

Just before 9:05 AM, about the time frozen on Ira McNabb's smashed clock, the *Mont Blanc* exploded in a huge cloud of molten metal, unleashing a wave of percussion more forceful than anything wrought by humankind before detonation of the atomic bomb.

Death and Destruction

In barely an instant, almost all of Richmond was destroyed, and much of the surrounding North End suffered devastation. A violent wave of percussion swept up and over Needham Hill, levelling buildings, crushing and trapping victims, and causing overturned stoves to ignite fires, transforming ruins into crematoria. A tsunami, or tidal wave, pulsed up the hill as high as sixty feet (18.3 metres), then receded, clawing people and wreckage back into the harbour. An oily, black cloud descended, raining shards of red-hot metal like projectiles out of hell. While most of the *Mont Blanc* blew to smithereens, its 1200-pound anchor blew to the Northwest Arm two miles away. Imploding windows pummelled onlookers with glass that blinded them and sliced through their bodies, killing and maiming. Strangely, many survivors could not recall the sound or force of the actual explosion. Walter Nickerson, a crew member aboard the *Stella Maris*, regained consciousness holding another crew member stripped of everything but his underwear. William Wells, driver of the *Patricia*, found himself standing up completely naked and missing the muscles of his right arm. Other courageous men were less fortunate. Constant Upham, Edward Condon, Horatio Brannan, and Vincent Coleman all died in the explosion, as did almost all crew members of the *Patricia*, *Stella Maris*, and boats from the *Highflier* and *Niobe*.

DESTROYED RICHMOND WITH THE *IMO* ON THE OPPOSITE SHORE, 1917

NEEDHAM HILL FROM THE WATERFRONT, C.1917

Hundreds of dazed survivors, many clutching blood-gushing wounds, began to search for their loved ones, help others, or simply wander the streets, where they saw corpses hanging out of windows and tangled in telegraph wires overhead. A rumour that the nearby Wellington Barracks munitions magazine might explode caused panic, and many survivors did their best to flee to open spaces as far away as Point Pleasant and the Northwest Arm. By noon, the threat of this explosion had passed, and the survivors trekked back to what was left of their properties. To make matters worse—if that seems possible—a fierce winter storm blew in and raged into

WRECKED RICHMOND HOME, C.1917

SEARCHING WRECKAGE IN FRONT OF HILLIS AND SONS FOUNDRY, C.1917

COLLAPSED DOMINION TEXTILES FACTORY, C.1917

NORTH STREET STATION WITH COLLAPSED ROOF, C.1917

the night, dumping 16 inches (40.6 centimetres) of snow on Halifax, freezing bodies, and hampering rescue efforts. In *Barometer Rising*, novelist Hugh MacLennan describes the scene the following morning:

> When dawn broke, Fort Needham looked like a long whale-back, pocked with hundreds of hummocks gray with sooty snow. But a fume of steam rose from the whole of it and blew southwest in the gale, and the thin line of men working methodically across it appeared like the vanguard of an attacking army stopped in its tracks digging in under fire.[5]

According to eyewitnesses, the death and destruction in Richmond exceeded the carnage of trench warfare in Europe.

The explosion did not spare homes, institutions, or businesses. Blown away or damaged beyond repair were the Richmond and North Street railway stations, Acadia Sugar Refinery, Hillis and Sons Foundry, and Dominion Textiles plant, where scores of workers were killed by collapsed machinery and floors. Gone too were all four Richmond churches, which lost a total of nearly 900 members. At the time of the explosion, classes at Richmond School on Roome Street had not quite begun, so, despite destruction of the building, only two students died there, although eighty-six other students died at home or on their way to school. Eight girls died at St. Joseph's School, along with fifteen girls absent from school and fifty-five boys scheduled to attend class that afternoon. Also hard hit was the Protestant Orphanage on Veith Street, reduced to rubble with heavy loss of life.

WRECKED GROVE PRESBYTERIAN CHURCH, C.1919

WRECKED RICHMOND SCHOOL ON ROOME STREET, C.1917

Statistical summaries of the death and destruction vary and, as new information becomes available, will continue to vary. One summary is 2,000 deaths, 1,600 destroyed buildings, 12,000 damaged buildings, 6,000 homeless people, 25,000 people with damaged homes, and $35 million worth of property damage. These numbers contrast with a toll of 650 deaths in the famous Chicago fire and San Francisco earthquake combined.

Rescue and Temporary Relief

At the time of the Explosion, Halifax mayor Peter Martin was out of town, but deputy major Henry Colwell, chief of police Frank Hanrahan, and lieutenant governor Grant MacCallum managed to confer. Officials and citizens met at City Hall and formed a series of Halifax Relief Committees to oversee emergency transportation, shelter, food, and money. Within three hours of the explosion, the army and navy had assumed power in the devastated area, restricted civilian access, and begun to search for survivors and recover bodies. The committees found emergency shelter for people at locations around the city, while the Engineering and Ordnance Corps erected emergency tents on the Halifax Common. When relief supplies arrived, the committees helped distribute them at available locations, including the Halifax

CHILDREN CARRYING RELIEF SUPPLIES, C.1917

SURVIVORS WAITING FOR FOOD AT THE HALIFAX ARMOURIES, C.1917

MEDICAL RELIEF TEAM FROM MASSACHUSETTS OUTSIDE BELLVUE HOSPITAL, c.1917

RELIEF NURSES OUTSIDE BELLVUE HOSPITAL, c.1917

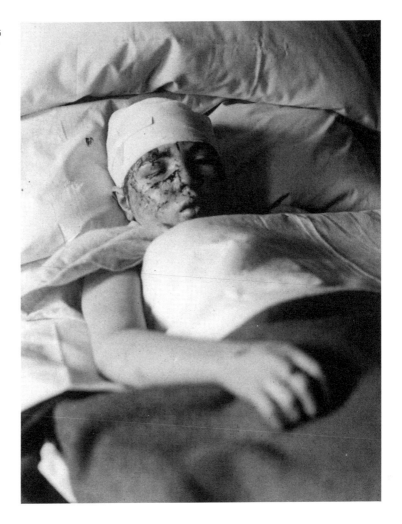

Armouries, where people stood in long lines awaiting food. A temporary hospital in
the YMCA building on Barrington Street received wounded adults and children,
many of them suddenly orphaned. When the Protestant Orphanage was relocated
and then rebuilt, some of the orphans were transferred there. Besides these organizations, individual Haligonians took advantage of any opportunity to provide assistance. Train 10, warned by Vincent Coleman, felt the explosion in Rockingham but
was able to proceed as far as Africville, where passengers, including architect
Andrew Cobb, disembarked into chaos, finding people shrieking, sobbing, and
burning alive. Train 10 later carried evacuees to Truro, arriving at about the same
time the first relief train arrived in Halifax, where passengers had to disembark at
Rockingham and trudge the rest of the way into town.

Devastated Halifax benefitted from the generosity of numerous individuals,
organizations, and governments. Of all these contributors, probably none remains
dearer to the hearts of Haligonians than the American state of Massachusetts. The
explosion destroyed lines of communication, so news of the disaster was slow to get

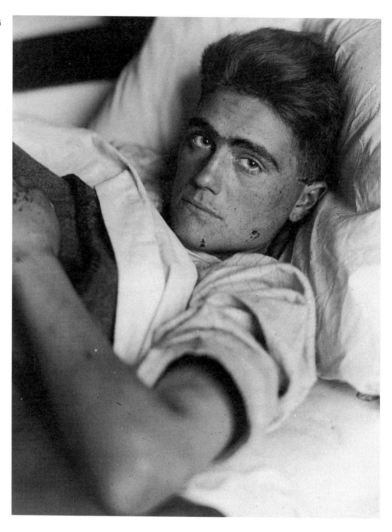

out. Massachusetts governor Samuel McCall managed to get word that same morning and immediately pledged assistance. By 10 PM, a train with doctors, nurses, and Red Cross workers departed Boston for Halifax. The train picked up relief workers and supplies along the way but was delayed by the raging snowstorm before arriving in Halifax at 3 AM on December 8. The train proceeded to the new South End terminals. It took four hours to reach the South End, where the group conferred with Canadian prime minister Sir Robert Borden, who had been attending a meeting on Prince Edward Island and made his way to Halifax largely by sleigh. The Massachusetts contingent then proceeded to City Hall to meet local officials, including members of the Halifax Relief Committees.

Officials granted the Massachusetts contingent use of Bellvue, an old mansion on Spring Garden Road. The building was in bad shape, but military personnel cleaned it up, and by 9 PM that night an operating room was in place, as well as a ward with a hundred beds, already occupied by sixty patients. By the next day, the

PROTESTANT ORPHANAGE DINING ROOM, AUGUST 15, 1918

American Bellvue Hospital was up and running, flying an American flag. The hospital treated the worst medical cases, taking pressure off other hospitals, especially Camp Hill, which had a capacity of 300 patients but was forced to admit 1,600. Convalescing patients were a heart-wrenching and pitiful sight.

In Boston, Governor McCall formed a Massachusetts–Halifax Relief Committee, which appealed for public donations. On December 9, the steamship *Calvin Austin*, loaned to the committee by the American government, sailed for Halifax with a $300,000 cargo of relief supplies, including badly needed window glass and crews of glaziers, wreckers, and workmen. A second steamship, the *Northland*, sailed on December 11 with a $250,000 cargo of motorized trucks, gasoline, and drivers. All these donations occurred during wartime, when goods and workers were in short supply. Later, when relief turned to reconstruction, the people of Massachusetts continued to be of great help. Since then, each year Haligonians express their gratitude by donating a huge Christmas tree to Boston, illuminated in a ceremony of remembrance.

UNIDENTIFIED DEAD OUTSIDE CHEBUCTO ROAD SCHOOL MORTUARY, DECEMBER 17, 1917

ROMAN CATHOLIC SERVICE FOR UNIDENTIFIED DEAD, DECEMBER 17, 1917

REMEMBERING UNIDENTIFIED PROTESTANTS AT FAIRVIEW CEMETERY, 1920S

Burying the Dead

In the immediate aftermath of the explosion, several locations around the city became temporary morgues, later consolidated into a mortuary in the basement of Chebucto Road School. Military personnel and volunteers were in charge of the mortuary, where they stripped and washed bodies, stored belongings in bags, and posted the names of those identified and the descriptions of those not. Helping them was future author Thomas Raddall, a student who collected water from neighbours to use in mortuary practice. Troops continued to remove bodies from wreckage until January 11, 1918, but long before then the mortuary became overcrowded, so unidentified victims had to be commemorated and buried.

On December 17, 1917, funerals for ninety-five unidentified victims took place in the Chebucto Road School yard. A throng of 3,000 mourners assembled, extending two blocks along the school building. Soldiers brought wreath-covered caskets from the basement and arranged them in rows for public view. Using associated personal effects, the mortuary workers had done their best to determine whether victims were Roman Catholic or Protestant or some other religious denomination. The Protestant commemorative service took place first, led by the

Anglican Archbishop of Nova Scotia, followed by the Roman Catholic service, led by priests of St. Joseph's Parish. The caskets were then put on trucks and driven in the company of hundreds of mourners to two cemeteries, the Roman Catholics to Mount Olivet Cemetery, and the others, mostly Protestant, to Fairview Cemetery. With each casket numbered, and its place of burial noted, identification later was still possible. Burials continued in this manner until Christmas Eve.

By February 1918, workers at the mortuary had processed hundreds of bodies. Workers processed more bodies at other locations, and crews found still more bodies in the coming months, as the ground thawed and they cleared away rubble. One survivor decided to search the ruins of his house by himself. What remained of his mother, two sisters, and brother he carried away in a shoebox.

Laying Blame

Initially unaware of what caused the Explosion, many Haligonians feared an attack by German Zeppelins, and, after they learned the true cause, some still suspected a German conspiracy. German residents of Halifax were temporarily imprisoned, and a few were stoned. After the First World War ended, some North End German families changed their surnames to disguise any association with the tragedy. There was also resentment of the French. Just a few months earlier, Quebec had resisted military conscription, provoking in English Canada accusations of lack of patriotism. Captain From of the *Imo* died in the Explosion, but Captain Le Medec survived and, having abandoned ship, was targeted with so much hostility that he sought police protection. Haligonians were hurt, angry, and bewildered, and they wanted, if not blood, at least answers and the laying of blame.

On December 12, 1917, less than one week after the disaster, an inquiry began in Halifax, presided over by Justice Arthur Drysdale. At the inquiry, Charles Burchell represented the owners of the *Imo*. Hearing no credible evidence of German involvement, he interrogated Captain Le Medec and pilot Mackey and aggressively sought to establish their guilt. Altogether, the inquiry heard testimony from more than fifty witnesses. On February 4, 1918, Justice Drysdale delivered his findings. He found Le Medec and Mackey responsible for violating navigational rules, recommending that France revoke Le Medec's license and prosecute him in accordance with French law. He recommended that Mackey be dismissed, his licence revoked, and that he be criminally prosecuted. Drysdale also found Le Medec and Mackey guilty of failing to warn the public of imminent danger, and he found Commander Frederick Wyatt, the naval officer in charge of harbour traffic, guilty of failing to enforce navigational rules. Le Medec and Mackey were arrested immediately, and Wyatt was arrested the following day, when all three men were charged with manslaughter. Owing to insufficient evidence, the charges against Le Medec and Mackey were dismissed, and Wyatt was acquitted.

Meanwhile, the owners of the *Imo* and *Mont Blanc* sued one another for $2 million. Legal proceedings began on March 7, 1918, also presided over by Justice Drysdale, who again held the *Mont Blanc* responsible for the collision. The owners of

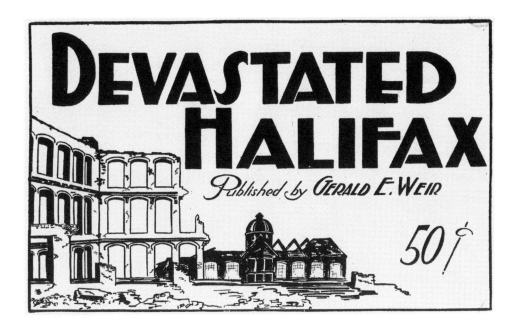

ADVERTISING VIEWS OF THE EXPLOSION, C.1918

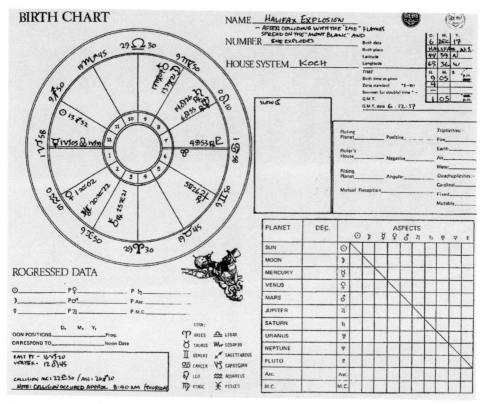

ASTROLOGICAL CHART OF THE EXPLOSION, C.1918

the *Mont Blanc* appealed to the Supreme Court of Canada, which, in a split decision, changed Drysdale's finding. A further appeal to the Privy Council in London produced a final decision that both ships were equally at fault. Francis Mackey remained in Halifax and returned to his job as a harbour pilot, Aimé Le Medec avoided censure by the French government and resumed his career, and Frederick Wyatt relocated to another naval post. The *Imo* was refloated, repaired, renamed, and reused as a whaling ship. On December 3, 1921, it ran aground off the Falkland Islands and sank. As might be expected, for devastated Halifax and thousands of victims, none of these outcomes provided "closure."

Explosion Fascination

Fascination may not be quite the right word to characterize the tremendous public interest in the Halifax Explosion, because, considering the impact of the tragedy, the word implies morbid curiosity, and this is rarely the case. But the word does capture the great breadth and depth of curiosity that has made the explosion almost legendary. Why such fascination? One answer is that the explosion was so momentous and touched the lives of so many people, who, only one or two generations removed, are able to perpetuate it as oral history. When the topic of the explosion arises in conversation, many North Enders can respond immediately with an anecdote about how it affected them, friends, or relatives. Another answer is that the explosion was an event of almost unparalleled magnitude with both tragic and heroic dimensions, so, like the sinking of the *Titanic* five years earlier, it looms human and at the same time larger than life. Then too, because the explosion was accidental, it seems to demand a more satisfying explanation, a lesson for the future, or the attribution of deeper meaning. Some fascination with the explosion derives from a shallow mentality that feeds mass-media sensationalizing of natural and human catastrophes. In contrast, the interest of numerous scholars and historians is sophisticated and genuine. They know that it is difficult to study the explosion and remain detached and unmoved.

In addition to public and private remembrances, the explosion has inspired articles, books, comics, conferences, documentaries, exhibits, films, monuments, novels, paintings, plays, photographs, sculptures, websites, and miscellaneous other explorations. There is so much interest in the explosion that some scientists and historians have undertaken to expose "myths" and misconceptions about it. People

PAINTING OF THE EXPLOSION FOR *TRUE MAGAZINE*, 1958

might believe, for example, that the explosion cloud was shaped like a mushroom (untrue), that there were actually several explosions (untrue), that the explosion caused a tidal wave (true, but it did not rise as high as Fort Needham, as some accounts claim), or that the explosion left a crater in the bottom of the harbour (possibly true, but there is no geological evidence.) Three photographs sample the more popular and esoteric interest. One photograph advertises a collection of pictorial views, another shows an undated and unsigned astrological chart, and a third shows provincial archivist Charles Bruce Fergusson, on the left, displaying a painting commissioned for *True* magazine. The painting is clearly inaccurate.

Chapter 9

Rebuilding the North End

GOVERNOR MCCALL APARTMENTS, OCTOBER 9, 1918

Temporary Housing

Because the Halifax Explosion occurred during wartime, on January 22, 1918, the Canadian government created the Halifax Relief Commission under authority of the War Measures Act. The initial members of the commission were T. Sherman Rogers, William Wallace, Frederick Fowke, and Ralph Bell. The commission took charge of the unfinished work of the earlier Halifax Relief Committees and their unspent donations. The

RECONSTRUCTION WORKERS NEAR THE EXHIBITION GROUNDS, 1918

MASSACHUSETTS–HALIFAX RELIEF COMMITTEE WAREHOUSE, 1918

FIRST FURNISHED GOVERNOR McCALL APARTMENT, 1918

province gave it sweeping authority to spend the donations to relieve and restore the most devastated areas of Halifax. Besides administering pensions, compensation, and medical and social services, the commission built temporary housing and developed a master plan to rebuild the North End.

Temporary housing was needed urgently to replace emergency shelters improvised in the days after the Explosion. The buildings on the Exhibition Grounds had suffered severe damage, so the Commission decided to raze them and use the grounds for temporary apartments. The commission hired hundreds of workers to commence construction. Within one month, the workers completed forty two-storey buildings with 320 apartments. The Governor McCall Apartments, named in honour of the Massachusetts governor, were tarpaper-covered wood with a life expectancy of five years. By mid-March, they were full of 2,200 tenants paying rents of $5–$12 per month. Furnishings came from the Massachusetts–Halifax Relief Committee, which maintained a warehouse on nearby Windsor Street. Tenants visited the warehouse to make their own selection, taking away beds, blankets, bureaus, and even baby carriages. In further recognition of the generosity of Americans, streets within the apartment complex bore the names of New England states.

The Hydrostone District

Exercising its authority to expropriate properties and rebuild, the Relief Commission hired urban planner Thomas Adams to redesign 325 devastated acres (131.6 hectares) in the North End. Adams, an Englishman working in Ottawa, espoused the "garden city" philosophy of urban planning, wherein, to make cities liveable, urban areas should incorporate green elements of the country. Assisted by architect George Ross of the Montreal firm of Ross and MacDonald, Adams devised a master plan with three aims: realign and improve old Richmond roads; build high-quality, attractive, and affordable permanent housing; and enhance new residential areas with parks and open spaces. Implemented, this vision became the first planned urban community in Canada.

For housing, Adams first set his sights on Merkelsfield, the flat and low-lying area west of Fort Needham bounded by Gottingen, Isleville, Young, and Duffus streets. Prior to the explosion, the Halifax Land Company had developed this area with roads and scattered two-storey, flat-roofed wooden houses. The Relief Commission expropriated land in Merklesfield and razed the ruined houses to make way for a bold new Hydrostone project. It got underway in September 1918, despite an initial reaction that the project was extravagant. The project took its name from its primary building material, Hydrostone, a Chicago company trade name for what were basically concrete blocks. The blocks were molded under pressure, cured with steam, and then faced with crushed granite or sand that made them sparkle. Stucco bonded well to their surface, and, at 80 pounds (36.3 kilograms) each, they could be lifted and laid without the need for expensive wall forms or cranes. Most important, they were fire-resistant, a quality highly desired after the explosion. A factory in Eastern Passage manufactured up to 4,000 blocks per day and then transported them on a specially constructed narrow-gauge railway to

URBAN PLANNER THOMAS ADAMS (1871–1940)

GOTTINGEN STREET ALONG FORT NEEDHAM, JULY 17, 1918

THE HYDROSTONE DISTRICT FROM FORT NEEDHAM, OCTOBER 7, 1918

CABOT PLACE FROM GOTTINGEN STREET, APRIL 21, 1919

MANUFACTURING HYDROSTONES, JANUARY 8, 1919

the Dartmouth waterfront, where they were shipped across the harbour and put on another railway directly to the construction site. Both Adams and designer George Ross touted Hydrostone as a building material of the future.

The Hydrostone district comprised ten blocks with 328 units of between four and one half to seven rooms each. Most of the units were linked in blocks of four or six, like townhouses, although there were a few two-unit blocks near Gottingen and Isleville streets. The exteriors of the units blended Hydrostone, wood, and stucco in a few patterns repeated with slight variation. With dormers, high-pitched roofs and wooden lattice, they looked Tudoresque, reminiscent of Thomas Adams's home country, England. On most streets, the units faced one another across broad boulevards planted with grass and trees, preserving natural light and fresh air and providing common playgrounds for children. Underground conduits for lighting kept the streetscapes free of unsightly poles, while common rear alleyways provided parking and servicing and concealed power and telephone lines. Befitting a project that did not want to lose sight of the past while looking forward to the future, some Hydrostone streets, such as Hennessey and Stairs, bore names of revered Haligonians, while others, such as Cabot and Columbus, bore names of explorers.

Some Hydrostone units opened in 1919, and the project was completed by 1921. About 2,000 tenants moved in, most of them from temporary housing, and

HARRY TAYLOR, 17 KANE PLACE, OCTOBER 19, 1923

HALIFAX RELIEF COMMISSION OFFICE AT YOUNG AND ISLEVILLE STREETS, EARLY 1920s

PAVING YOUNG STREET AT GOTTINGEN, c.1920s

paid rents averaging $25 per month. One proud tenant was Harry Taylor, who by 1923 had landscaped the front yard of 17 Kane Place and installed a flag pole flying the Canadian Red Ensign. Along Young Street, facing a small triangular park, the Hydrostone district showcased a string of neighbourhood offices and enterprises. In 1921, there were eleven such establishments, including, at the corner of Gottingen Street, the Royal Bank and North End Pharmacy and, at the corner of Isleville Street, the office of the Halifax Relief Commission.

With 2,000 residents, the Hydrostone district nurtured neighbourhood pride and a desire for neighbourhood improvements, including paved streets. A photograph shows workers paving Young Street in front of the Royal Bank and North End Pharmacy. In the background, a picket fence borders Saul Mosher's property on the site of old Linden Hall.

The Hydrostone district evolved into a family-oriented community with the sort of neighbourliness captured in the photograph of the Jean Fong and George Seto wedding party at the corner of Young and Isleville streets around 1947. The groom owned the Tea Garden Grill, an eatery no longer standing. The Halifax Relief Commission managed the Hydrostone units until 1949, when it began selling them for between $2,500 and $3,500 each, completing sales by 1955. In the hyper-inflationary 1970s, the district was one of the first in the North End to gentrify with a new breed of North Ender driven there by skyrocketing house prices elsewhere. The Young Street commercial strip remained largely ungentrified until the 1990s, when Larex Properties bought most of the buildings and redeveloped them as the upscale Hydrostone Market.

JEAN FONG AND GEORGE SETO WEDDING PARTY AT YOUNG AND ISLEVILLE STREETS, C.1947

Rebuilding Elsewhere

When Ross and MacDonald unveiled plans for the Hydrostone district, despite earlier doubts, North Enders were impressed and lobbied the architects to build houses elsewhere, focusing on the slopes of Fort Needham. There the firm of Cavicchi and Pagano employed 450 workers clearing away debris, a job that was largely completed by June 1918, leaving the area stripped, scarred, and uninviting.

On these slopes, Thomas Adams wanted new roads to follow natural geographical contours. He created Devonshire and Dartmouth avenues as broad boulevards running at 45 degree angles to the axis of the peninsula. Devonshire

RICHMOND SQUARE AND SCHOOL, SEPTEMBER 20, 1921

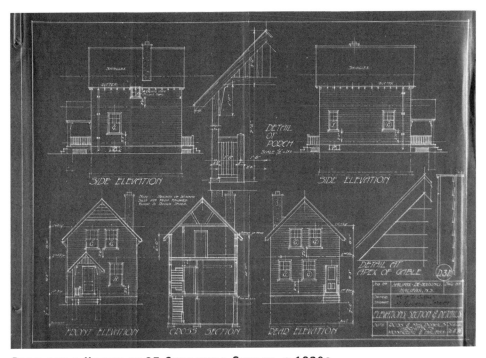

PLAN FOR A HOUSE AT 37 COLUMBUS STREET, C.1920S

BUILDING A HOUSE AT 42 LIVINGSTONE STREET, AUGUST 19, 1918

ran northwest from Barrington Street toward Gottingen, while Dartmouth, which he envisioned as a route to a future Halifax harbour narrows bridge, ran northeast from Gottingen Street toward Barrington. The two avenues crossed in an X shaped-formation at old Acadia Square, sometimes called Richmond Square, which Adams reserved for public buildings. By 1921, Richmond School had been rebuilt at the square, and students resumed classes while trying to normalize their lives. Architect Andrew Cobb, who had seen the effects of the explosion first-hand, designed the school, which bears a plaque dedicated to the memory of former students killed. Today the school building houses a provincial court. On occasion, employees report hearing the ghosts of children past.

With Merklesfield occupied by relatively densely populated Hydrostones, Adams thought that the slopes of Fort Needham would support more spacious lots with roomier single-family houses. Ross and MacDonald designed several house plans using combinations of Hydrostone, stucco, shingle, and wood. Especially popular was their plan for 37 Columbus Street, repeated in houses along Roome Street north of Richmond Square. The Relief Commission also built a small community of houses northeast of Young Street and Longard Road (Robie Street), including the house at 42 Livingstone Street photographed under construction.

REBUILT FORMER RICHMOND, 1930s

Altogether, Ross and MacDonald designed more than 600 houses built by the Relief Commission outside the Hydrostone district. Now interspersed among newer houses, they constitute an impressive legacy of post-explosion rebirth.

The Relief Commission expected that it would seed the slopes of Fort Needham with houses, then private investment would take over. But the North End was depopulated, and many North Enders had horrible memories of the area, were superstitious, and refused to move back. Furthermore, in the 1920s Halifax suffered a severe economic recession, followed a decade later by the Great Depression. An aerial photograph of the area in the 1930s shows that in places it was less crowded than before the explosion. Real growth of this part of the North End did not resume until the prosperity and population pressure of the Second World War.

FORT NEEDHAM BEFORE LANDSCAPING, C.1950

Fort Needham Becomes a Park

Thomas Adams envisioned Fort Needham as a showcase public park in the North End that would rival Point Pleasant Park in the South End. With other important responsibilities, the Relief Commission was unable to concentrate on Fort Needham until 1949, when it began to divest itself of other properties. By then it had made some minor improvements to the hill, but, except for a panoramic view, it was far from attractive. The hill was littered with rocks and scrub vegetation, and its high water table caused unsightly erosion along Gottingen Street.

In August 1949, the Relief Commission and the City of Halifax signed an agreement to develop Fort Needham Park. They agreed that the commission would landscape and otherwise improve the park at its own expense, then turn it over to the city, which would maintain it for the public—forever. The commission worked intermittently for the next ten years, spending more than $150,000 on grading, planting, sports and recreational facilities, and a canteen. This work destroyed the remains of Fort Needham redoubt, visible in the 1930s aerial photograph but now covered by tennis courts. In 1959, by mutual agreement, Fort Needham was hand-ed over to the city, and in 1980, city council enacted building height restrictions to protect its view of ground zero of the explosion.

Fort Needham Memorial Park is dedicated to victims of the Halifax Explosion, but until 1984 it lacked a suitable monument. There were small monuments scattered around the city, including the site of the *Mont Blanc* anchor and a metal sculpture in front of the Halifax North Memorial Library. But none of these monuments was grand, so a group of citizens began raising money for a $400,000 memorial carillon on top of Fort Needham. The carillon, formally dedicated in 1985, houses bells donated to Kaye Street United Memorial Church in memory of members of the Orr family who died in the Explosion. Made of a material like Hydrostone, the imposing carillon straddles former Richmond Street, which descends almost directly to where the *Mont Blanc* blew up. Each year on the morning of December 6, survivors gather to remember the catastrophe and observe a moment of silence.

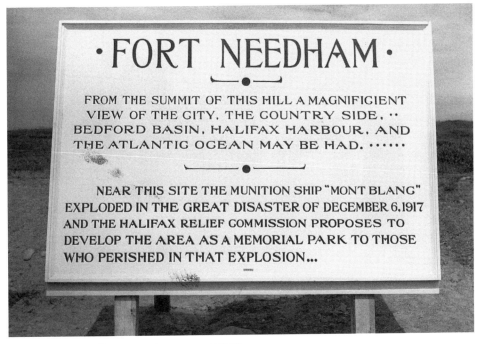

THE VISION OF THOMAS ADAMS, C.1950S

HALIFAX EXPLOSION MEMORIAL CARILLON, 1986

Chapter 10

Saga of Africville

AFRICVILLE BEFORE RELOCATION, PRE-1970

Black Settlement around Halifax

Black Haligonians have settled around the city for a variety of reasons. In early Halifax, black slaves were sold at public auctions and through advertisements in newspapers. Slavery in Nova Scotia ended officially in 1808, twenty-five years before the British Crown abolished it throughout the Empire. During the American War of Independence, the Crown promised American slaves their freedom if they would help fight the rebellious colonies. When the Crown lost the war, it evacuated about 2,300 black Loyalists and 1,200 black slaves of white Loyalists to Nova Scotia. The colony granted them marginal rural land that proved difficult to farm, and in 1792, about 1,200 of these evacuees left for Sierra Leone. In 1795, a group of black Maroons revolted against the British colonial government of Jamaica. To rid themselves of this threat, the Crown deported them to Nova Scotia. Some Maroons worked on Citadel Hill, and others worked on the estate of governor John Wentworth, but most settled temporarily in rural Preston, where, like their predecessors, they found life marginal. In 1800, the Crown re-deported the Maroons to Sierra Leone.

The last major influx of black settlers occurred around the time of the War of 1812. During the war, many black Americans fled to British ships and were evacuated to Nova Scotia as refugees, about 1,200 of them landing in Halifax. Largely destitute and unhealthy, they lived for a while in the Halifax Poor House and in emergency quarters on Melville Island in the Northwest Arm. About a hundred remained in Halifax, while the rest joined ex-slaves and Loyalists in the struggling black communities of Preston and Hammonds Plains. There they too found the soil infertile and the location removed from opportunities for wage labour. When the Crown abolished slavery, white authorities worried that Nova Scotia would experience a flood of new black refugees. This flood never materialized, but in anticipation of it, the colony withheld assistance to the refugees already arrived. As a result, the residents of Preston and Hammonds Plains remained desperately poor for a long time, not receiving legal title to their land until 1842, after they had lived on it for more than a generation.

Traditionally, most black Haligonians have lived in the North End, beginning not only in Africville but also around Maynard and Creighton streets. Black Haligonians have owned property around Maynard and Creighton for more than 150 years, going back to when the streets developed out of Maynard's and Creighton's fields. Early on, black students there attended a neighbourhood philanthropic African School, and later, when provincial legislation allowed the city to exclude blacks from common schools, separate black schools were built elsewhere. On paper, racial separation remained a Halifax school policy until 1954.

Whatever their original religious affiliation, most black Haligonians became Baptists, inspired by David George, an American ex-slave, and John Burton, the English founder of the first Halifax Baptist Church. In 1832, following changes in congregation, the church emerged as the Cornwallis Street African Baptist Church, with charismatic Richard Preston as pastor. In the years leading up to the American Civil War, Preston preached against the evils of American slavery and worked with New Englanders for its abolition. In 1854, he organized the Nova Scotia African Baptist Association, with the Cornwallis Street church as its head. Ever since, the Church has been a spiritual and social centre for black North Enders.

Origin and Evolution of Africville

The precise origins of Africville are unclear, but the community dates back to at least the 1840s, when it was settled by members of the Brown family, including William, John, and Thomas Brown. The first documented property transaction was a purchase by William Brown in 1848. Three years later, the community had eighty residents, most of them refugees or descendants of refugees from the War of 1812 who had drifted toward Halifax looking for work. Earlier residents may have helped construct Campbell Road. For a while, the community was known by the name Campbell Road, but the name Africville was used regularly after 1900. Africville began on three 5-acre (2.0 hectare) lots at the tip of the Halifax peninsula along Bedford Basin. It never expanded much beyond 15 acres (6.1 hectares), so, as its population increased, the lots became smaller and more important to be preserved through inheritance.

Remote from Halifax, Africville endured indignities, inconveniences, and dangers that would have been considered intolerable in town. In 1854, the Nova Scotia Railway split the community in half, and later, two other railway lines, including the Cotton Company spur line, passed within feet of homes. Some Africville men earned modest wages as railway conductors, but all residents

AFRICVILLE, EARLY 1960S

endured terrible community hazards. Spewing smoke as they passed noisily through, trains menaced residents, injuring and killing several, including children who chased trains to retrieve lumps of coal to heat their family homes. After 1900, the city cited this "unsightly" route as a reason for re-routing the railway to the South End.

In 1858, the city located its "night soil" depository near Africville, and at about the same time, it built Rockhead Prison on a bluff 1,000 yards away. In the 1870s, it moved the Infectious Diseases Hospital near the prison and added to raw sewage already draining into Bedford Basin. Besides all this, Africville was encroached upon by huge power transmission towers, oil storage tanks, a coal-handling facility, a fertilizer manufacturing plant, and a slaughterhouse. The *coup de grace* came in the 1950s when the city relocated its open refuse dump a stone's throw away. A shocking speculation is that Africville residents experienced so much contamination that they developed immunities to diseases to which other Haligonians succumbed.

Despite crippling impositions, Africville evolved into a vibrant community. It acquired a school, postal outlet, and a church. For decades, Seaview African United Baptist Church was the heartbeat of the community, staging demonstrative Sunday services, including a colourful sunrise service on Easter followed by spectacular baptisms in the waters of Bedford Basin. A rocky bluff spared Africville from the full

SEAVIEW AFRICAN UNITED BAPTIST CHURCH, 1950S OR 1960S

INFECTIOUS DISEASES HOSPITAL, C.1935

ROCKHEAD PRISON, 1929

ROAD TO AFRICVILLE, 1917

force of the Halifax Explosion, and only a handful of residents died. A 1917 photograph shows Africville women in the aftermath of the explosion walking along Campbell Road. Later, when the road became Barrington Street and was partially paved, an Africville resident recalled, "When the pavement ends, that's where Africville begins."

After World War One, as deprivations mounted, the social fabric of Africville began to unravel, and the stabilizing influence of the church waned. Some residents deserted the community, while undesirable outsiders moved in to engage in illicit activities, notably bootlegging. During the Second World War, Africville acquired a reputation as a destination for after-hours drinking and partying. After the war, when the community attracted more notoriety, Haligonians became increasingly uncomfortable about it. In the 1960s, Africville came under intense scrutiny that brought this discomfort to a head.

The Faces of Africville

People can see what they want to see or can be selective in what they consider important. The observations of outsiders can be superficial, while those of insiders can offer a different perspective. It is unsurprising, then, that as Africville came under increasing scrutiny, opinion about it divided.

As late as 1960, although Africville had electricity and telephones, almost all of it lacked piped water and sewers. City officials argued that bedrock made water and sewers prohibitively expensive and that residents were in arrears paying taxes. Residents counter-argued that bedrock did not prevent the provisioning of water

AFRICVILLE, EARLY 1960S

AFRICVILLE CHILDREN, DECEMBER 1947

UNSAFE WATER, C.1950S

SALVAGING THE DUMP, C.1950S

GEORGE DIXON.

and sewers elsewhere and that, without these services, their taxes were unfairly high. Meanwhile, the lack of water hydrants made fires in Africville especially dangerous. City officials were also relaxed about enforcing building codes in Africville, with the result that parts of the community appeared dilapidated. When officials did attempt enforcement, some residents accused them of enforcing a double standard, ignoring equivalent or worse infractions elsewhere. Images of badly peeling paint, outhouses, heaps of scrap metal, and abandoned cars allowed Haligonians to brand Africville a shanty town or slum, a stereotype reinforced by images of children huddled together to avoid winter cold. Two of the most unflattering images of

Africville showed a contaminated well and salvagers at the adjacent city dump.

On the other hand, observers who knew Africville well, residents and visitors alike, touted the resilience and success of the community, which nurtured bantamweight and featherweight world boxing champion George Dixon. Many Africville homes, while perhaps modest, were respectable and thoroughly capable of supporting wholesome family life. With music, especially religious music, so important to the community, some homes had pianos or other musical instruments. On occasion, musician Duke Ellington visited Africville, home of the father of his wife, she who inspired the song *Sophisticated Lady*. Seen in the proper light, life in Africville looked enjoyable, even idyllic, as residents went about their daily business, shopping at the penny store, picking blueberries, or simply climbing the hill above the shining waters of Bedford Basin. These were some of the memories that residents cherished after their community was destroyed.

Climbing the Hill, c.1950s

The Blueberry Patch, c.1950s

MATILDA NEWMAN'S STORE, 1950S OR 1960S

Grant, Ted / Library and Archives Canada / e002283006

DAN DIXON'S HOME, 1950S OR 1960S

Grant, Ted / Library and Archives Canada / e002283007

Relocation

By about 1960, attitudes and events came together to seal Africville's fate. This was the era of racial integration, a politicized movement aimed at eliminating racial segregation in housing, schooling, and economic opportunity. It was also the era of post-Second World War urban renewal, when cities across North America razed "blighted" neighbourhoods and moved inhabitants into new public housing. Often accompanying these trends was the attitude that government knew what was good for people better than the people knew themselves.

In the 1950s, the city hired Gordon Stephenson, professor of town and regional planning at the University of Toronto, to chart its course for urban renewal. Stephenson recommended that Africville be removed, identifying its land as valuable for future industry. In 1961, the city formed a Department of Development, and the following year the department also recommended removal. The department proposed that residents with legal title to their land be compensated $500, and those without legal title negotiate compensation or, if negotiation failed, seek redress in court. In August 1962, politicians and Africville residents attended a meeting at Seaview African Baptist Church, where residents rejected proposed relocation strongly. Some of them sought help from the National Committee on Human Rights, which sent lawyer Alan Borovoy to Halifax. His visit led to the formation of the Halifax Human Rights Advisory Committee to act as liaison between the department and residents. Most committee members considered the removal of Africville almost inevitable and concentrated on trying to obtain better financial deals for those affected.

RELOCATION MEETING AT SEAVIEW CHURCH, AUGUST 23, 1962

CITY OFFICIALS VISITING AFRICVILLE, C.1960S

DEACON RALPH JONES'S BOARDED-UP HOUSE, C.1960S

In 1963, the Advisory Committee recommended that Albert Rose, professor of social work at the University of Toronto, visit Halifax to offer advice. Rose spent three days in the city—and two hours in Africville. In agreement with Stephenson and Borovoy, he recommended relocation, suggesting a two to three year time frame and financial assistance with job training, welfare, and legal aid. He also recommended that the Department of Development hire a social worker to facilitate relocation arrangements. The Advisory Committee and City Council both accepted the Rose report, and on January 9, 1964, at a meeting of Africville residents, it was accepted by thirty-seven of forty-one in attendance.

By and large, relocation followed the process envisioned by Rose and other consultants. In 1964, the city hired social worker Peter MacDonald, who began visiting homes and establishing rapport with relocatees. Within one month, he negotiated the first relocation deal: a resident without title to her land received $500, free moving, accommodation in public housing, and cancellation of an outstanding $1500 hospital bill. As each new deal was concluded, the city quickly boarded up a building and demolished it, chipping away at the community, making it less inviting, and encouraging those remaining to move. Especially upsetting was the bulldozing of Seaview Church, the heart and soul of a community then in the throes of death.

By the end of 1967, almost everybody in Africville was gone, 80 families and 400 people, some of them, such as Dorothy Carvery, moved out in dump trucks. As relocation progressed, the City began to reconfigure the tip of the North End with new highways and the A. Murray MacKay narrows bridge. In late 1969, the last remaining Africville resident, Aaron "Pa" Carvery, stood in the way of the

RELOCATING DOROTHY CARVERY, c.1960s Grant, Ted / Library and Archives Canada / e002283009

Grant, Ted / Library and Archives Canada / e002283008

bridge approach. Carvery had been dickering with the city since 1966 without success. In late December, city officials summoned him downtown for an encounter, which he later described.

> They sent for me and when I got there I was taken into someone's office. There was five or six persons in the room plus a suitcase full of money all tied up neatly in bundles. The suitcase was open and stuck under my nose so as to tempt me and try and pay me off right there and then.[6]

Upset, Carvery responded by recounting the incident in the *Halifax Mail-Star*. Nevertheless, on December 30, he settled for $14,387.76. On January 2, 1970, Carvery moved, and four days later his house was demolished and paved over for a road. One of the ironies of the Africville saga is that the city ended up paying $550,000 for the land, with an additional $200,000 budgeted for relocation assistance. This total approximated its earlier $800,000 estimate for upgrading Africville services, an estimate it declared prohibitively expensive.

Remembering Africville

Africville residents moved to various locations, mainly around the North End. Some moved to public housing at Mulgrave Park, while additional public housing was under construction at Uniacke Square. A few of them enjoyed their bright, new accommodations, but almost all missed the outdoor scenery, fresh ocean breezes, and community togetherness. Other residents became homeowners, although several had difficulty with more expensive upkeep. Still others rented accommodations, but many of these accommodations were substandard and slated for demolition, so residents again had to move. Government bureaucracy foiled some residents trying to receive promised social assistance and trapped others, overwhelmed by new financial responsibilities, in a welfare net. Another Africville irony is that, before relocation, ten percent of residents received welfare, while after relocation, the number swelled to fifty percent.

In 1967, Dalhousie University professor Donald Clairmont proposed to study the Africville relocation project, believing that it might serve as a model for relocations elsewhere. By the time he published his study as a book, he had changed his mind and become critical of its heavy-handedness and technocratic manipulation. As negative consequences of relocation mounted, retrospective assessment of the project shifted. Sympathy for former residents increased, and residents themselves acted to perpetuate the memory of their community, in 1983 forming the Africville Genealogical Society.

In 1991, the province announced that a planned road would encroach on the site of demolished Seaview Church.

ARCHAEOLOGISTS EXCAVATING THE FOUNDATION OF SEAVIEW CHURCH, NOVEMBER 1992

REUNION OF FORMER AFRICVILLE RESIDENTS, SEPTEMBER 13, 1986

To honour the memory of Africville, the province agreed to fund the design and construction of a nearby church replica. With input from the Genealogical Society and the Technical University of Nova Scotia, consultants decided that an archaeological assessment was called for. In November, 1992, archaeologist Katie Cottreau-Robins and a team of investigators, including volunteers from Halifax West High School, excavated the church foundation, recorded architectural features, and retrieved artifacts, notably a long, hand-painted sign that read "God is Love." Fourteen years later, the replica had not yet been built.

A final Africville irony is that its former location, once touted for industrial development, has ended up a tax-exempt city park. Seaview Memorial Park opened in 1985 on 25 acres (10.1 hectares) of land overlooking Bedford Basin, where each summer the Genealogical Society stages a ceremonial homecoming. In 1986, former Africville residents met at the North Branch Library on Gottingen Street to reminisce and discuss how Africville might otherwise be remembered. Two years later, a monument dedicated to the community was erected at Seaview Park. The monument bears a poetic inscription.

> To lose your wealth is much
> To lose your health is more
> To lose your life is such a loss
> That nothing can restore.

Chapter 11

The Second World War

WARTIME CONVOY IN BEDFORD BASIN, EARLY 1940S

"An East Coast Port"

The end of the First World War hit Halifax extremely hard. Besides coping with the aftermath of the Halifax Explosion, the city endured a decade-long post-war economic recession, followed in the 1930s by the Great Depression. There was little time, and less money, to rehabilitate deteriorated buildings and infrastructure before rumblings of a new war with Germany began. A harbinger of war was the dirigible *Hindenberg*, which on July 4, 1936, cruised low over the North End, possibly photographing the dockyard. On September 3, 1939, Britain declared war on Germany, and a short time later Canada followed suit. Within two weeks, the apparatus of war once again commandeered Halifax.

It is difficult to overstate the impact of the Second World War on Halifax, especially to Haligonians who did not experience it first-hand. In wars involving Europe and North America, the city has always been strategically important, straddling the great circle route across the North Atlantic and offering an expansive, protected harbour for ships. During the Second World War, 368,000 Canadian army men and women crossed the North Atlantic on a hundred different ships, including the refitted *Queen Elizabeth*, which alone carried 14,000 troops. Almost all of these ships left Canada from Halifax.

In 1940, prime minister W. L. Mackenzie King appointed Nova Scotia premier Angus L. Macdonald federal minister in charge of building a Canadian navy. At the time, the navy comprised six destroyers, four minesweepers, and fewer than 1,700 personnel. Within two years, Macdonald had expanded it to 300 ships and 36,000 personnel. Much of this expansion took place in the North End at the Naval Dockyard and Shipyards.

GOVERNOR GENERAL, THE EARL OF ATHLONE, VISITING THE DOCKYARD, JUNE 21, 1941

At the start of the war, the dockyard still bore evidence of its eighteenth-century origins, occupied by quaint old ironstone and wooden buildings. Modernization swept these buildings away and replaced them with facilities suitable for what became the third-largest naval fleet in the world. The modernized dockyard employed up to 3,000 civilians, while 20,000 naval men and women occupied facilities at Wellington Barracks, the old Exhibition Grounds, and Willow Park. The navy established its administrative headquarters at the old Prince Edward Hotel on North Street, renaming it HMS *Canada*. On occasion, wartime Governor-General of Canada the Earl of Athlone visited the dockyard to inspect ships and boost morale. Meanwhile, equipped with a huge new floating drydock, the Halifax Shipyards built ships for Canada and repaired ships from around the world, many of them crippled by German torpedoes. Working feverishly around the clock, the shipyards and the dockyard repaired an astonishing wartime total of 7,000 vessels. Exempt from a ban on bright nighttime lights, the shipyards shone eerily far out to sea, seen by lurking German submarines, from whom Haligonians contemplated imminent attack.

The main job of the Canadian Navy was to patrol the North Atlantic and make it safe for convoys to and from Europe. This job was crucial to the Allied effort, especially after the United States joined the Allies in 1941. As in the First World

CONVOY CONFERENCE AT ADMIRALTY HOUSE, MARCH 1941

War, departing convoys assembled in Bedford Basin, where they presented a panorama of hulking grey metal. The day before departure, the Naval Control Officer convened a convoy conference, often at Admiralty House, where he assigned each ship a place in the convoy and told the captains when they would weigh anchor and what secret signals they were to use en route. Altogether, during the war, 57,000 ships cleared Halifax harbour, an average of twenty-six every day for six years. These figures lend credence to the claim that Halifax then may well have been the most important port in the world.

The wartime stresses and strains on Halifax exceeded those of any other city in North America. The population of the peninsula more than doubled, and in places it was awash in uniforms, especially in the North End, where the navy paraded down Barrington and Brunswick streets to attend church. Uniformed men and women competed with ordinary Haligonians for food, shelter, clothing, and scarce entertainment, depleting supplies and driving up prices. Overcrowding was epidemic, with houses packed to the rafters and hotel rooms resembling dormitories. Taxicabs were scarce, as were tramcars, which had to be imported from other cities. More tramcar tracks were needed, but metal was in short supply, so tracks were torn up at Point Pleasant Park and reinstalled on north Gottingen Street.

NAVAL CHURCH PARADE ALONG BARRINGTON STREET, C.1945

NAVAL CHURCH PARADE ◦ ST PATRICKS CATHOLIC CHURCH
J. HAYWARD 11 BUCKINGHAM ST

NAVAL CHURCH PARADE ALONG BRUNSWICK STREET, C.1945

Halifax never saw battle, but the threat of attack from sea and air was omnipresent. The harbour was protected by submarine booms and curtailed by German mines, with ships sinking only five miles out to sea. Searchlights strafed the sky, sirens wailed, and aircraft patrolled overhead. In order to supply departing ships with water, the supply to homes was cut off, and when the Dockyard and Shipyards needed more power, homes endured brownouts and blackouts. Sometimes food was so scarce that Haligonians trying to be hospitable to service personnel could offer them little more than conversation or a comfortable chair. Throughout the War, the extent of these threats and deprivations remained unknown to most Canadians, who, with censorship and secrecy, received news about Halifax only as the anonymous "An East Coast Port."

AIR RAID PRECAUTIONS (ARP) PLATOON 9 HEADQUARTERS AT AGRICOLA AND MACARA STREETS, OCTOBER 30, 1942

OPENING OF AIR RAID PRECAUTIONS PLATOON 9 HEADQUARTERS AT AGRICOLA AND MACARA STREETS, OCTOBER 30, 1942

Civilian Defense

For six years during the war, Haligonians felt under siege, if not physically, then mentally, having to be in constant readiness for possible enemy attack. The civilian defense force was the Halifax Civil Emergency Corps, directed by Major Osborne R. Crowell. The corps comprised numerous divisions mobilized to detect and combat air raids and fires, rescue victims, administer first aid, distribute water, and demolish wrecked buildings. By the end of 1943, it had enlisted 6,000 members. Because the corps was worried about incendiary bombs, it established an Air Raid Precautions (ARP) network modelled after a similar network in besieged London. In 1942, the corps ordered every household in Halifax to stockpile bags of sand to fight fires, distributing 1.5 million pounds of sand for this purpose. It recommended that Haligonians buy gas masks, and when retailers such as Eaton's Department Store received supplies, they advertised them in newspapers. Even in an age of global violence, Canadians today imagine such precautions only in other, war-torn countries.

In the North End, one of the most active ARP units was Platoon 9, with a cross-section of the neighbourhood population, including businesspeople, labourers, and students. Fifty-four platoon wardens used $900 of their own money, their

AIR RAID PRECAUTIONS PLATOON 7, SECTION E2, FIRE WATCHERS, BETWEEN GERRISH AND CUNARD STREETS, JULY 8, 1943

STAGING RESCUE AND FIRST AID ON YOUNG STREET, JUNE 21, 1943

own labour, and discarded airplane crates to construct their headquarters at the corner of Agricola and Macara streets. The photograph of the official opening on October 30, 1942, shows some of the wardens along with Major Crowell seated at the far right next to Mayor W. E. Donovan. The wardens met once a week for business, once a week with volunteers, and once a week to socialize, cementing personal bonds that long outlasted the war. Personal bonds also characterized Air Raid Precautions Platoon 7, Section E2, which monitored Creighton, Maynard, and Gottingen streets between Gerrish and Cunard. The photograph of the Section on July 8, 1943, shows commanding warden Walter Johnson standing third from the left on the porch. In front, fire watchers (FW) display their stirrup water pumps, the kind used in London during the German *blitzkrieg*.

In the evening of June 21, 1943, Air Raid Precautions staged a mock air raid over Halifax with demonstrations at thirty mock incidents. With the city truly blacked out, at a building on Young Street, a rescue squad extended a ladder to the second floor, rigged a block and tackle, and evacuated a man supposedly wounded. Meanwhile, at the corner of Charles and Creighton streets at the rear of Joseph Howe School, fire watchers fought a supposed fire with buckets and a stirrup pump. While these and other demonstrations were going on, airplanes dropped 20,000 leaflets that warned "This might have been a bomb." Where else in Canada were the perils of the war brought so close to home?

DEMONSTRATING A WATER PUMP AT CHARLES AND CREIGHTON STREETS, JUNE 21, 1943

Prefabricating North End Houses, 1941

Assembling Prefabricated Houses, 1941

Wartime Housing

At the start of the war, large parts of the far North End were still sparsely settled, especially north of Duffus Street and Lady Hammond Road. The northwest of the peninsula, overlooking Bedford Basin and Africville, was occupied by Rockhead Prison and farms of families such as the Longards and Mersons. The northeast of the peninsula, also overlooking the Basin and Africville, presented another face to the industrialized harbour of former Richmond. For a long time, this area had been Anglican glebe land bordering the governor's North Farm. Some of it developed before the Halifax Explosion, but it suffered in the explosion and remained largely beyond the reach of redeveloper Thomas Adams. Even south of Duffus Street, on the old North Farm, owing to a shrunken economy and population, the in-fill housing envisioned by Adams had failed to materialize, leaving much of the area green. It was predictable, then, that when the government looked for land for wartime housing, it found plenty of it available in the far North End.

The Dominion government built two kinds of wartime housing in the far North End. South of Duffus Street in Mulgrave Park, it built rows of two-storey wooden barracks for the military, while north of Duffus on former glebe land, it built streets of single-storey prefabricated wooden bungalows for wartime workers. The bungalows, called "prefabs," were also scattered around the West End, but they were more conspicuous climbing up the steep North End slope on streets such as Glebe, Vestry, and St. Paul's, names that recall an Anglican past.

The wartime housing was designed to be only temporary, with the prefabs expected to last a maximum of twenty years. Within this time, the military barracks

BARRACKS AND PREFABS, 1941

MILITARY BARRACKS AT MULGRAVE PARK, 1941

in Mulgrave Park were demolished and the area occupied by public housing. In 1950, after considerable debate, the city of Halifax bought the prefabs from Central Mortgage and Housing Corporation for $1,000 each and arranged to sell them on the open market. Many of them were then rented by war veterans. Because the prefabs lacked proper foundations and chimneys, a condition of sale was that the city or owners add these improvements. As a result, the prefabs have long outlived their twenty-year life expectancy and now constitute a distinctive, suburban-looking North End neighbourhood.

MISHAP ON AGRICOLA STREET, JUNE 4, 1941

The V-E Day Riots

As the war dragged on, the mutual tolerance of Haligonians and their uniformed guests wore thin. Lines were long, shortages rife, and inconveniences great. The 1941 photograph shows one small example—a tramcar on Agricola Street derailed by a collision with a Bren-gun carrier. Increasingly, Haligonians complained about overcrowded stores and restaurants, as well as the rowdy behavior of soldiers and sailors. For their part, soldiers and sailors found Halifax boring, and they resented the price-gouging of landlords, taxi drivers, and retailers. A special target of resentment was the Nova Scotia Liquor Commission, which severely rationed the sale, consumption, and distribution of alcohol. During the war, with ration coupons, the maximum anyone could buy was two quarts of diluted gin, one quart of diluted rum or whiskey, or two quarts of diluted beer—per month. Anyone buying alcohol was expected to take it home immediately by the shortest possible route and was prohibited from giving it to another person, even a spouse. It was illegal to carry an open bottle of alcohol or to drink it outdoors, even at home. Alcohol was banned from military barracks, and the few bars in town charged prices that the average army and navy personnel could ill afford. Needless to say, ration books became a hot commodity on the black market and bootlegging a profitable way of life.

In spring 1945, with Allied victory in Europe near, Halifax military and civilian authorities began to prepare for victory celebrations. Authorities worried about how

LOOTING THE LIQUOR COMMISSION ON HOLLIS STREET, MAY 8, 1945

thousands of armed service personnel might release pent-up emotions. Radios in Halifax broadcast news of the surrender of Germany on May 7 at 10:30 A.M. Whistles blew, and thousands of people streamed onto streets to celebrate. Because authorities had recommended that bars, restaurants, and theatres close, crowds milled around without much to do. At 9 P.M., the wet canteen at HMCS *Stadacona* also closed, and a rowdy crowd of sailors, half-drunk, swept outside and tried to commandeer a tramcar on north Barrington Street. A shore patrol managed to disperse the crowd, but it headed downtown to join revellers in pulling wires off tramcars, smashing their windows, and setting one tramcar on fire. Hundreds of revellers broke into a Liquor Commission store, then, at midnight, moved on to two others, looting them. At 1 A.M., when the police arrived, the melee subsided, as if, suddenly, everybody was shocked to realize it had begun.

The morning of May 8 arrived tense but relatively calm, with many Haligonians unaware of the unrest of the previous night and many more preparing to enjoy the official V-E Day celebrations on the Halifax Common. At 1 P.M., the wet canteen at Stadacona ran out of beer, and another rowdy crowd spilled out onto north Barrington Street, commandeered another tramcar, ejected its passengers, vandalized it, and drove it downtown. Accompanying them was a group of up to 2,000 people who smashed windows along both sides of Barrington Street. As word of renewed unrest spread, sailors were joined by civilians who deserted the official celebrations for ones that offered greater thrills. A huge crowd attacked a Liquor Commission store with a battering ram, and an even larger crowd broke into Keith's Brewery. Streets grew deep with glass from smashed windows as mobs cleaned out stores and stashed loot in locations they were too drunk to remember

MAYHEM ON SALTER STREET, MAY 8, 1945

STRIPPING A MANNEQUIN, MAY 8, 1945

when they sobered up. Some women stole jewelry and fur coats, while others disrobed to have sex with sailors on Citadel Hill. Some photographs of the mayhem were too explicit for mass circulation. Others showed sailors exposing the private parts of a partially clothed female mannequin.

At 6 PM, authorities imposed a curfew, and by midnight the worst of the riot was over, with many rioters rounded up, dispersed, or staggering back to their barracks and homes. The aftermath was 3 deaths, 211 arrests, and 564 looted businesses, with the loot including 65,000 quarts of liquor and 8,000 cases of beer. When Haligonians learned the true extent of the disturbance, they felt angry and ashamed. With so many civilians participating, they had to shoulder some of the blame themselves. The mayor blamed the navy, while the navy blamed bootleggers. A committee of the Privy Council held an official inquiry and blamed the navy for failing to keep its servicemen off the streets. When a Royal Commission reached a similar conclusion, the federal government awarded victims $3 million in compensation. The V-E Day riots soured relations between the navy and the city, tarnished the reputation of everyone involved, and were an ignominious end to six otherwise praiseworthy years of service and sacrifice for Canada and Allied nations.

RIOT AFTERMATH ON BARRINGTON STREET BETWEEN JACOB STREET AND BELL LANE, MAY 1945

The Second Halifax Explosion

Constant wartime traffic in Halifax harbour kept alive memories of the 1917 explosion. Although regulations governing traffic had improved, there was still a risk of accident. In fact, during the Second World War, there were several close calls. On April 9, 1942, fire broke out aboard the British munitions ship *Trongate*, which burned into the early hours of the following morning before being scuttled by the minesweeper *Chedabucto*. On November 3, 1943, the American freighter *Volunteer* caught fire, threatening its potentially deadly cargo: 500 tonnes of light ammunition; 1,800 tonnes of heavy howitzer ammunition, depth charges, and dynamite; and 2,000 drums of combustible magnesium. Fortunately, the *Volunteer* was towed to McNab's Island, beached, and its fire extinguished. With scares such as these, when Allied victory in Europe arrived, Haligonians breathed a special sigh of relief.

As it turned out, their relief was premature. After the 1917 explosion, when the munitions magazine at Wellington Barracks threatened to explode, the magazine had been closed and a new magazine opened on the eastern shore of Bedford Basin. After V-E Day, ships returning to Halifax unloaded their unused ammunition at the Bedford magazine, which became so crowded that some ammunition had to be stored outside near a jetty. On July 18, 1945 at around supper time, an ammunition barge at the jetty exploded in a blast that shook the North End. The blast

BEDFORD MAGAZINE EXPLODING JULY 18–19, 1945

ignited exposed ammunition, sending up a huge cloud of smoke and unleashing a string of reverberations and fireworks similar to those that had enticed unsuspecting residents of Richmond to watch the burning *Mont Blanc*.

At 9 PM, with the reverberations and fireworks unabating, the navy ordered everyone north of North Street to evacuate their homes, later expanding the order to include everyone north of Quinpool Road. Because the route off the peninsula at Bedford Basin was unsafe, most people evacuated by the route along the Northwest Arm, causing a miles-long jam of automobiles with hastily gathered household valuables lashed to their tops. Many other residents stayed in their homes, and many evacuated only to Point Pleasant or Citadel Hill, where they could watch the spectacle over the North End nighttime skyline. On the evening of July 19, the evacuees, by then 15,000 strong, were allowed to return home, where they found shattered windows and cracked plaster as far south as downtown.

Fortunately, only one person was killed in the second Halifax explosion, and damage was relatively minor. Haligonians praised the navy for heroic efforts to combat the fire and in the process forgot some of the bad feelings they harboured for the V-E Day riots. On August 14, 1945, Japan surrendered, the Second World War ended, and North Enders finally looked forward to well-deserved quiet and peace.

Chapter 12

Urban Renewal

LOOKING NORTH OVER ALMON AND YOUNG STREETS, 1949

Changing the Face of the North End

Stresses of the Second World War accelerated ongoing deterioration of Halifax infrastructure and buildings. Streets and street railways became dilapidated, and old houses were carved up into ramshackle apartments and rooms, destroying their architectural integrity and making parts of the North End look like a refugee-swollen city in Europe. Even before the war ended, the city realized that it had to plan for post-war renewal.

GOTTINGEN STREET AT CORNWALLIS, MARCH 12, 1949

BRUNSWICK STREET AT JACOB, C.1949

In 1943, the city created a Civic Planning Commission, which began work immediately and issued a landmark report in 1945. Bluntly optimistic, the report called for sweeping changes to downtown and the North End. To revitalize downtown, much of the "blighted" old north suburbs was to be razed for a swath of new superhighways to transport people to and from new commercial highrises. Lady Hammond Road was to be widened to link with Devonshire Avenue and Barrington Street in another superhighway downtown. Africville was to be removed and the Rockhead Prison lands developed with single-family homes. Because many people in the old north suburbs were poor, home ownership there was considered unrealistic, so it was to be developed with low-income rental housing.

After the war, the Canadian armed services handed over to the city parcels of land it had used for temporary housing and wartime operations. The photograph over Almon and Young streets in 1949 shows that wartime intrusion into this part of the North End had been widespread. On the left, along Windsor Street, was an ordnance depot, and along both Almon and Young streets were barracks for military personnel and families of returned veterans. Dismantling these facilities left the area open for post-war redevelopment, which has been so extensive that it is difficult to visually connect its appearances then and now.

In control of more land, the city could take better charge of shaping its post-war face. Also, by the mid-1950s, it was clear that Canada and allied nations faced a new kind of war, a cold war, which pumped money into Halifax for armed services preparedness. Avoiding its usual post-war economic slump, the city had greater ability, as well as confidence, to chart its own course. Seeking outside advice, it hired Gordon Stephenson, professor of town and regional planning at the University of Toronto, to follow-up the Civic Planning Commission and recommend a course of action.

Stephenson's 1957 report was highly touted. There were several planks to its platform for urban renewal. One was to raze the "slums" around Jacob Street, redevelop the area commercially from the ground up, and relocate hundreds of residents to new public housing at Mulgrave Park. Another was to convert Barrington Street into a multi-lane highway that would sweep along the waterfront connecting at major interchanges to widened east-west highways. Stephenson had big plans for the old north suburbs, which he characterized as rife with physical and social problems, measured by high incidences of substandard buildings, fires, social welfare, juvenile delinquency, and crime. Reflecting attitudes then widespread, he believed that solving the physical problems would solve the social problems. In other words, eliminating "slum" buildings would eliminate "slum" behavior.

Stephenson was appalled by conditions along Upper Water and north Barrington streets, which, according to him, would make an "unworthy" approach from the Angus L. Macdonald harbour bridge to a gleaming new downtown. The bridge, which connected to North Street, had opened to traffic in 1955. Exiting motorists were encouraged to travel downtown via Gottingen Street, "the people's street," still bustling with friendly neighbourhood establishments such as the Vogue cinema and Saks. To capitalize on this high-traffic advantage, Stephenson

INAUGURATING THE ANGUS L. MACDONALD BRIDGE, APRIL 1955

VOGUE CINEMA, 46 1/2 GOTTINGEN STREET, MAY 10, 1948

SAKS, 114 GOTTINGEN STREET, JANUARY 8, 1949

urged that buildings behind Gottingen Street be demolished to make room for parking cars. To speed along demolition, he recommended strict enforcement of Ordnance 50, a controversial new city by-law that set minimum acceptable standards for housing.

The city attempted to implement almost all of Stephenson's recommendations, proceeding further with some than with others. In 1958, with great fanfare, municipal, provincial, and federal governments announced joint plans to redevelop downtown. By 1962, most of the area around Jacob Street had been razed and its residents relocated to Mulgrave Park. On the site rose Scotia Square, a complex of concrete office, commercial, and residential high rises begun in 1966 and completed ten years later. Public opinion about Scotia Square was mixed, with some Haligonians praising it as a wave of the future and others criticizing it for unwisely obliterating the past. One predicted consequence was that Scotia Square attracted business from the vicinity and hastened the decline of Gottingen Street.

The city drew battle lines in the community when it began to build Harbour Drive, a multi-lane, limited access highway modelled on the East Side Highway in New York. For Harbour Drive, it demolished almost every building on both sides of Barrington Street between North Street and downtown—the route Gordon Stephenson deemed unworthy. At first, the drive was to run the entire length of Halifax peninsula, all the way through downtown and Point Pleasant to connect

SAKS INTERIOR, JANUARY 8, 1949

with a bridge across the Northwest Arm. The initial phase of projected construction involved three large traffic interchanges at Devonshire Avenue, North Street, and Cogswell Street. Construction of the Cogswell Interchange caused the demolition of most of the old ordnance yard north of downtown. Extending the drive south of the yard would have required demolition of more waterfront buildings along Upper Water Street. The threat to these buildings galvanized community opposition to the ongoing massive demolitions. Spared the wrecking ball, the buildings became Historic Properties, which blocked Harbour Drive and made the Cogswell Interchange only quasi-functional.

With Scotia Square for corporations and Harbour Drive for commuters, the city embarked on something grand for North Enders themselves—Uniacke Square. The square was a self-contained urban village located between north Gottingen and Brunswick streets, necessitating demolition of the Institution for the Deaf and Dumb. Construction began in 1964 and continued for several years, yielding an inner-city community of highrise and lowrise residences furnished with a school, post office, library, and recreation centre named in honour of George Dixon.

To make room for Uniacke Square, the city demolished buildings along the west side of Brunswick Street from near Cornwallis Street to North. A few years later, when construction of Brunswick Towers threatened buildings on the east side of Brunswick, the Halifax Landmarks Commission and the Heritage Trust of Nova

OLD NORTH SUBURBS AND DOWNTOWN BEFORE DEMOLITION, C.1960

Scotia convinced the city to save a few of them for future generations. Meanwhile, opponents of Harbour Drive lobbied for green space around Brunswick Towers, forcing the towers to intrude into Barrington Street in the "Barrington bubble."

By the early 1970s, urban planners had left whole blocks of the North End gap-toothed and then filled the gaps with the kind of low-income housing recommended by Gordon Stephenson, notably Uniacke Square, Brunswick Towers, and senior citizen highrises. Despite these efforts, or maybe because of them, the North End continued to suffer. Shopping malls in the West End took people away from downtown, and more affordable housing in the suburbs drained people off the peninsula. Redevelopment was spotty and slow, as empty lots and boarded-up buildings made areas in transition uninviting. North of Duffus Street, Rockhead Prison closed, and private investors rebuilt the site with townhouses, apartments, and condominiums. South of North Street, however, the concentration of low-income people took money away from neighbourhood businesses, created social stigma, and added to economic difficulties. Between 1961 and 1976, the population of the North End declined forty-two percent.

What reversed this decline? In the 1970s, Haligonians began to realize that earlier schemes for urban renewal had been partially counterproductive, and, as a result, efforts to renew the North End took a different turn. A successful neighbourhood improvement program allowed homeowners to make their own improve-

OLD NORTH SUBURBS AND DOWNTOWN AFTER DEMOLITION, EARLY 1960S

ments. Housing cooperatives and community-based initiatives led to rehabilitation and rebuilding in the area around Uniacke Square. Significantly, the 1978 Municipal Development Plan, contrasted with the earlier Stephenson plan, sought to preserve neighbourhood integrity, blend old and new, and solicit community involvement.

Yet the real reason the North End turned around probably had little to do with any planned effort. In the 1970s, global shortages of gasoline, hyper-inflation, and mortgage rates as high as eighteen percent brought house hunters back to the peninsula and forced them to look in neighbourhoods they otherwise might not have considered. Soon a new breed of North Ender ventured in, living cheek-by-jowl with old-timers while rehabilitating houses dubbed "fixer-up-ers." Gentrification of the North End began first in the far north, then in the Hydrostones and surrounding area, and last, owing to its checkered reputation, in the neighbourhood just north of Citadel Hill. Despite initial trepidation, many new residents took a liking to the North End and were reluctant to cash in their equity and leave. Favourable word of mouth spread, and, once a critical mass was achieved, gentrification accelerated. It continued throughout the buoyant 1980s, the recessionary 1990s, and the city-wide building boom at the beginning of the new millennium.

Old-timers are probably amused to see new-timers discover the advantages of North End living, because old-timers have known about these advantages all along. One unfortunate disadvantage, however, is that, owing to accident and intent, much of the North End is physically disconnected from its past, making it difficult to understand how it came to be. A proper understanding of that past should inspire pride. For more than 250 years, contrasted with other Haligonians, North Enders have lived lives significantly beyond their own control, lives scripted by adversity and the decisions of more influential people. Pride, then, comes from merely surviving, adapting, and playing major supporting roles on the world stage.

Endnotes

1 Quoted in Thomas H. Raddall, *Halifax: Warden of the North*, rev. ed. (McClelland and Stewart, 1971), 148.
2 Charles Dickens, *American Notes* (Collins' Clear-Type Press, n. d.), 39.
3 Nova Scotia Archives and Records Management, MG 100, Vol. 153, No. 23.
4 Nova Scotia Archives and Records Management, MG 100, Vol. 87, No. 35.
5 Hugh MacLennan, *Barometer Rising* (Sloan and Pearce, 1949), 292.
6 Quoted in the *Halifax Mail-Star*, January 12, 1970, 5.

References

Articles, Books, Chapters, Reports, and Theses

Africville Genealogical Society. *The Spirit of Africville*. Halifax, Nova Scotia: Formac Publishing Company, 1992.
"Africville Remembered." In *Halifax's North End: An Anthropologist Looks at the City*, by Paul A. Erickson, 119-122. Hantsport, Nova Scotia: Lancelot Press, 1986.
Africville: The Spirit that Lives On. Halifax, Nova Scotia: Mount Saint Vincent Art Gallery, Africville Genealogical Society, Black Cultural Centre for Nova Scotia, and Atlantic Centre of the National Film Board, 1989.
Akins, Thomas Beamish. *History of Halifax City*. 1895 Reprint. Belleville, Ontario: Mika Publishing, 1973.
Beed, Blair. *The Halifax Explosion and American Response*. Halifax, Nova Scotia: Dtours Visitors and Convention Service, 1998.
Bell, Winthrop. *The "Foreign Protestants" and the Settlement of Nova Scotia*. Toronto, Ontario: University of Toronto Press, 1961.
Bird, Michael J. *The Town that Died: The True Story of the Greatest Man-Made Explosion Before Hiroshima*. Toronto, Ontario: Ryerson Press, 1962.
Blakeley, Phyllis. "The Forgotten Father of Confederation—and Pioneer of the Intercolonial Railway." *Atlantic Advocate* 59(5): 38-43 (January 1969).
Blakeley, Phyllis. *Glimpses of Halifax, 1867–1900*. 1949 Reprint. Belleville, Ontario: Mika Publishing, 1973.
A Brief History of the Little Dutch Church. Halifax, Nova Scotia: Morton & Company, 1899.
Brown, Robert. *"Halifax Birney Stronghold." Canadian Historical Association Incorporated Bulletin 17* (1954).
Brunswick Street Feasibility Study. Halifax, Nova Scotia: MacFawn and Rogers, 1969.
Cadera, Lori. "VE Day Riots Halifax, May 7-8, 1945." *Trident* 12(9): 1-4 (May 4, 1978).
Campbell, Margaret. *No Other Foundation: The History of Brunswick Street United Church and Mission with its Methodist Inheritance*. Hantsport, Nova Scotia: Lancelot Press, 1984.
Chambers, Robert W. *Halifax in Wartime: A Collection of Drawings*. Halifax, Nova Scotia: The *Halifax Herald* and the *Halifax Mail*, 1943.
Civic Advisory Committee on the Preservation of Historic Buildings. *Brunswick Street, a Survey of Buildings and Environs*. Halifax, Nova Scotia: City of Halifax, 1968.

Clairmont, Donald H. *Africville: The Life and Death of a Canadian Black Community*. rev. ed. Toronto, Ontario: Canadian Scholar's Press, 1987.

Clairmont, Donald H. and Dennis W. Magill. *Africville: The Life and Death of a Canadian Black Community*. Toronto, Ontario: McClelland and Stewart, 1974.

Clairmont, Donald H. and Dennis W. Magill. *Africville Relocation Report*. Halifax, Nova Scotia: Institute of Public Affairs, Dalhousie University, 1971.

Clarke, Ernest. "The Hydrostone Phoenix: Garden City Planning and the Reconstruction of Halifax, 1917–21." *Ground Zero: A Reassessment of the 1917 Explosion in Halifax Harbour,* edited by Alan Ruffman and Colin D. Howell, 389–408. Halifax, Nova Scotia: Nimbus Publishing Limited and the Gorsebrook Research Institute of Saint Mary's University, 1994.

Collins, Louis W. "Brunswick Street—After Two Decades." *Halifax's North End: An Anthropologist Looks at the City,* by Paul A. Erickson, 115–118. Hantsport, Nova Scotia: Lancelot Press, 1986.

Comiter, Alvin and Elizabeth Pacey. *Historic Halifax*. Willowdale, Ontario: Hounslow Press, 1988

Dawson, Joan. *The Mapmaker's Eye: Nova Scotia Through Early Maps*. Halifax, Nova Scotia: Nimbus Publishing Limited and the Nova Scotia Museum, 1988.

DeVolpi, Charles P. *Nova Scotia A Pictorial Record: Historical Prints and Illustrations of the Province of Nova Scotia Canada 1605-1878*. Toronto, Ontario: Longman Canada Limited, 1974.

Dickens, Charles. *American Notes*. London, England: Collins' Clear-Type Press, no date.

Dictionary of Canadian Biography. Vol.XII S.v. "Akins, Thomas Beamish," by Brian Cuthbertson, 13–17.

Dictionary of Canadian Biography. Vol.VII S.v. "Campbell, Sir Colin," by Phillip Buckner, 142–145.

Dictionary of Canadian Biography. Vol. IX S.v. "Cunard, Sir Samuel," by Phyllis Blakely, 172-186.

Dictionary of Canadian Biography. Vol.XIII S.v. "Dixon, George," 276–278.

Dictionary of Canadian Biography. Vol.VIII S.v. "Kempt, Sir James," by Peter Burroughs, 458–465.

Dictionary of Canadian Biography. Vol.VI S.v. "Uniacke, Richard John," by Brian Cuthbertson, 789–792.

Dictionary of Canadian Biography. Vol.VI S.v. "Uniacke, Richard John," by Brian Cuthbertson, 792.

Edwards, Don and Devonna Edwards. *The Little Dutch Village: Historic Halifax West: Armdale, Fairview*. Halifax, Nova Scotia: Nimbus Publishing Limited, 2003.

Erickson, Paul A. *A Block of Time*. Halifax, Nova Scotia. Report to Cultural Resource Management Limited, 2003.

Erickson, Paul A. *All that Remains: The Saga of Human Burials Beneath the Little Dutch Church in Halifax*. Halifax, Nova Scotia: Report to the Nova Scotia Museum of Natural History, 1999.

Erickson, Paul A. *Halifax's North End: An Anthropologist Looks at the City*. Hantsport, Nova Scotia: Lancelot Press, 1986.

Erickson, Paul A. *Halifax's Other Hill: Fort Needham from Earliest Times*. Halifax, Nova Scotia: Department of Anthropology, Saint Mary's University, 1984.

Erickson, Paul A. and Graeme F. Duffus. *Carleton House: Living History in Halifax.* Halifax, Nova Scotia: Heritage Trust of Nova Scotia and Nimbus Publishing Limited, 1997.

Erickson, Paul A., Dawn Mitchell, Laird Niven, Katie Cottreau, and Nicola Hubbard. "Sellon Site (BdCv:7)." *Nova Scotia Museum Curatorial Report 63. Archaeology in Nova Scotia 1985 and 1986* (1987): 9–75.

Fader, Gordon. "Seabed Impacts of the Explosion of the *Mont Blanc.*" *Ground Zero: A Reassessment of the 1917 Explosion in Halifax Harbour*, edited by Alan Ruffman and Colin D. Howell, 345-364. Halifax, Nova Scotia: Nimbus Publishing Limited and the Gorsebrook Research Institute of Saint Mary's University, 1994.

Fingard, Judith, Janet Guilford, and Donald Sutherland. *Halifax: The First 250 Years.* Halifax, Nova Scotia: Formac Publishing Company, 1999.

Founded Upon a Rock: Historic Buildings of Halifax and Vicinity Standing in 1967. Halifax, Nova Scotia: Heritage Trust of Nova Scotia, 1967.

Haliburton, Gordon MacKay. *A History of Railways in Nova Scotia.* Masters Thesis, Dalhousie University, 1955.

Halifax and its Business: Containing Historical Sketch, and Description of the City and its Institutions; Also Description of Different Lines of Business, with Account of the Leading Houses in Each Line. Halifax, Nova Scotia: Nova Scotia Printing Company, 1876.

Halifax and its People: 1749-1999: Images from Nova Scotia Archives and Records Management. Halifax, Nova Scotia: Nimbus Publishing Limited, 1999.

Hill, George W. "Nomenclature of the Streets of Halifax." *Collections of the Nova Scotia Historical Society* 14: 1-22 (1910).

Hind, H. Y., et al. *The Dominion of Canada; Containing a Historical Sketch of the Preliminaries and Organization of Confederation.* Toronto, Ontario: L. Stebbins, 1869.

Hopkins, H. W. *City Atlas of Halifax, Nova Scotia.* Halifax, Nova Scotia: Provincial Surveying and Publishing Company, 1878.

Isaacs, I. J., compiler. *The City of Halifax: The Capital of Nova Scotia Canada: Its Advantages and Facilities.* Halifax, Nova Scotia: Halifax Board of Trade, 1909.

Kitz, Janet. "Halifax Explosion Memorial Bell Tower." In *Halifax's North End: An Anthropologist Looks at the City*, by Paul A. Erickson, 108-114. Hantsport, Nova Scotia: Lancelot Press, 1986.

Kitz, Janet. *Shattered City: The Halifax Explosion and the Road to Recovery.* Halifax, Nova Scotia: Nimbus Publishing Limited, 1989.

Kitz, Janet. *Survivors: Children of the Halifax Explosion.* Halifax, Nova Scotia: Nimbus Publishing Limited, 1992.

Kline, Bernard. "Post Cards of the 1917 Explosion." *Ground Zero: A Reassessment of the 1917 Explosion in Halifax Harbour*, edited by Alan Ruffman and Colin D. Howell, 139-161. Halifax, Nova Scotia: Nimbus Publishing Limited and the Gorsebrook Research Institute of Saint Mary's University, 1994.

Landmarks of the City of Halifax. Halifax, Nova Scotia: Halifax Landmarks Commission, 1971.

Lyman, George Hinckley. *The Story of the Massachusetts Committee on Public Safety February 10, 1917–November 21, 1918.* Boston, Massachusetts: Wright & Potter Printing Company, State Printers, 1919.

Mackenzie, Shelagh with Scott Robson, editors. *Halifax Street Names: An Illustrated Guide.* Halifax, Nova Scotia: Formac Publishing Company, 2002.

McCann, L. D. "Staples and the New Industrialism in the Growth of Post-Confederation Halifax." *Acadiensis* 8(2): 47-79 (1979).

Mellish, Annie Elizabeth. *Our Boys Under Fire: Canadians in South Africa*. Charlottetown, Prince Edward Island: Examiner Office, 1900.

Metson, Graham, compiler and editor, with Cheryl Lean. *An East Coast Port . . . Halifax at War 1939–1945*. Toronto, Ontario: McGraw-Hill Ryerson Limited, 1981.

Metson, Graham, editor. *The Halifax Explosion December 6, 1917*. Toronto, Ontario: McGraw-Hill Ryerson Limited, 1978.

Miller, Janice. "Halifax, Nova Scotia: A Study of the Effects of Disaster on Urban Morphology." In *Ground Zero: A Reassessment of the 1917 Explosion in Halifax Harbour* edited by Alan Ruffman and Colin D. Howell, 409-420. Halifax, Nova Scotia: Nimbus Publishing Limited and the Gorsebrook Research Institute of Saint Mary's University, 1994.

Millward, Hugh. *The Geography of Housing in Metropolitan Halifax, Nova Scotia*. Halifax, Nova Scotia: Department of Geography, Saint Mary's University, 1981.

Mitchell, Dawn T. "Digging the North End." In *Halifax's North End: An Anthropologist Looks at the City*, by Paul A. Erickson, 123–128. Hantsport, Nova Scotia: Lancelot Press, 1986.

Monnon, Mary Ann. *Miracles and Mysteries—The Halifax Explosion December 6, 1917*. Windsor, Nova Scotia: Lancelot Press, 1977.

Mortell, J. S. "The Achievements of Agricola and the Agricultural Societies, 1818–25." *Bulletin of the Public Archives of Nova Scotia* 2: 1-48 (1940).

Mullane, George. "Old Inns and Coffee Houses of Halifax." *Collections of the Nova Scotia Historical Society* 22: 1–23 (1933).

Nolan, Dave. "The RCR: A Century of Service." *The Atlantic Advocate* 73(10): 10-14 (1983).

Now It Can Be Told. Halifax, Nova Scotia: Nova Scotia Light and Power Company, 1946.

Pacey, Elizabeth. *Georgian Halifax*. Hantsport, Nova Scotia: Lancelot Press, 1987.

Pacey, Elizabeth. *Miracle on Brunswick Street: The Story of St. George's Round Church and the Little Dutch Church*. Halifax, Nova Scotia: Nimbus Publishing Limited, 2003.

Payzant, Joan M. and Lewis J. Payzant. *Like a Weaver's Shuttle: A History of the Halifax-Dartmouth Ferries*. Halifax, Nova Scotia: Nimbus Publishing Company, 1979.

Penny, Allen. *Houses of Nova Scotia: An Illustrated Guide to Architectural Style Recognition*. Halifax, Nova Scotia: Formac Publishing Company, 1989.

Piers, Harry. *The Evolution of the Halifax Fortress 1749–1928*, revised by G. M. Self under the direction of D. C. Harvey. Halifax, Nova Scotia: The Public Archives of Nova Scotia, 1947.

Power, L. G. "Richard John Uniacke." *Collections of the Nova Scotia Historical Society* 9: 73-118 (1895).

Punch, Terrence M. "The North End as a State of Mind." *Halifax's North End: An Anthropologist Looks at the City*, by Paul A. Erickson, 99–103. Hantsport, Nova Scotia: Lancelot Press, 1986.

Raddall, Thomas. *Halifax: Warden of the North*, rev. ed. Toronto, Ontario: McClelland and Stewart, 1971.

Redman, Stanley R. *Open Gangway: An Account of the Halifax Riots, 1945*. Hantsport, Nova Scotia: Lancelot Press, 1981.

Report on the Provincial Museum and Science Library for the Fiscal Year 1930–31. Halifax, Nova Scotia: Minister of Public Works and Mines King's Printer, 1932.

Report on the Provincial Museum and Science Library for the Fiscal Year 1935–36. Halifax, Nova Scotia: Provincial Secretary King's Printer, 1937.

Roberts, Leslie. *Canada: The Golden Hinge*. Toronto, Ontario: Clarke, Irwin and Company, 1952.

Robinson, Ernest Fraser. *The Halifax Disaster December 6, 1917*. St. Catherine's, Ontario: Vanwell Publishing Limited, 1987.

Ross, R. W. "What Church Union Will Mean for the City of Halifax." *The New Outlook* 1(1): 37 (June 1925).

Ruffman, Alan and Colin D. Howell, editors. *Ground Zero: A Reassessment of the 1917 Explosion in Halifax Harbour*. Halifax, Nova Scotia: Nimbus Publishing Limited and the Gorsebrook Research Institute of Saint Mary's University, 1994.

Ruffman, Alan and David Simpson. "Realities, Myths, and Misconceptions of the Explosion." *Ground Zero: A Reassessment of the 1917 Explosion in Halifax Harbour*, edited by Alan Ruffman and Colin D. Howell, 301–325. Halifax, Nova Scotia: Nimbus Publishing Limited and the Gorsebrook Research Institute of Saint Mary's University, 1994.

Ruffman, Alan, David A. Greenberg, and Tad S. Murty. "The Tsunami from the Explosion in Halifax Harbour." *Ground Zero: A Reassessment of the 1917 Explosion in Halifax Harbour*, edited by Alan Ruffman and Colin D. Howell, 327–344.. Halifax, Nova Scotia: Nimbus Publishing Limited and the Gorsebrook Research Institute of Saint Mary's University, 1994.

Schofield, Murrille. "Halifax Railway Stations 1860s–1970s." *Powergram* 3(5): 8–9 (May 1974).

Shutlak, Garry. "A Vision of Regeneration: Reconstruction After the Explosion, 1917–21." *Ground Zero: A Reassessment of the 1917 Explosion in Halifax Harbour*, edited by Alan Ruffman and Colin D. Howell, 421–426. Halifax, Nova Scotia: Nimbus Publishing Limited and the Gorsebrook Research Institute of Saint Mary's University, 1994.

Simpson, David and Alan Ruffman. "Explosion Bombs and Bumps: Scientific Aspects of the Explosion." *Ground Zero: A Reassessment of the 1917 Explosion in Halifax Harbour*, edited by Alan Ruffman and Colin D. Howell, 275–299. Halifax, Nova Scotia: Nimbus Publishing Limited and the Gorsebrook Research Institute of Saint Mary's University, 1994.

Smith, Marilyn Gurney. *The King's Yard: An Illustrated History of the Halifax Dockyard*. Halifax, Nova Scotia: Nimbus Publishing, 1985.

Smith, Marilyn Gurney. "Navy in the North End." *Halifax's North End: An Anthropologist Looks at the City*, by Paul A. Erickson, 104–107. Hantsport, Nova Scotia: Lancelot Press, 1986.

Sparling, Mary Christine. *The British Vision in Nova Scotia 1749–1848: What Views the Artists Reflected and Reinforced*. Masters Thesis, Dalhousie University, 1978.

Stephenson, Gordon. *A Redevelopment Study of Halifax, Nova Scotia*. Toronto, Ontario: University of Toronto Press, 1957.

Waring, Gerald. "Almost Forgotten South African Conflict Sped Canada's Evolution as a Nation." *The Standard*, July 15, 1950, 12–17.

White, James F. E. *The Ajax Affair: Citizens and Sailors in Wartime Halifax, 1939–1945*. Masters Thesis, Dalhousie University, 1984.

Withrow, Alfreda. *One City, Many Communities*. Halifax, Nova Scotia: Nimbus Publishing Limited, 1999.

Manuscripts, Newspapers, and Web Pages

All manuscripts belong to Nova Scotia Archives and Records Management.

Origin of the North Suburbs
Edward Cornwallis Revisits Halifax
Halifax Herald, August 7, 1924, 1. MG 100, Vol. 156, Nos. 12-12h.

Arrival of Foreign Protestants
Origin of Dutch Town
Halifax Mail-Star, May 7, 1952, 24, 28.
Thomas Beamish Akins and his Cottage
MG 100, Vol. 101, Nos. 9, 14.
A North End Success Story
Commercial News, October 1963, 23; *Halifax Chronicle*, June 16, 1941, 8; *Halifax Chronicle-Herald*, October 21, 1961, 5; *Halifax Mail*, June 16, 1941, 7; *Halifax Mail-Star*, May 2, 1960, 12, November 18, 1967, 1, 6; *Morning Herald*, July 16, 1880, 3. MG 9, Vol. 43, 128.

The Naval Dockyard
Admiralty House
Halifax Mail-Star, September 29, 1956, 1, February 8, 1963, 1, 6, March 18, 1972, 41. MG 100, Vol. 149, No. 15, Vol. 211, No. 28.
The Dockyard in Motion
O/S, V/F, Vol. 23, No. 19; V/F, Vol. 143, No. 10.

The Military Garrison
Wellington Barracks
Halifax Chronicle, February 7, 1948, 1.
The Halifax Armouries
Evening Mail, February 27, 1894, 5, December 19, 1894, September 28, 1896; *Halifax Herald*, September 29, 1896, June 28, 1899; *Morning Chronicle*, June 23, 1894.

Gradual Expansion North
Major North End Roads
Novascotian, August 23, 1836, 226.
A Famous Duel
Acadian Recorder, July 24, 1819, 3, July 31, 1819, 2. MG 1, Vol. 1769, Nos. 38–40, Vol. 2140, No. 154.
Arrival of the Cunards
Colonial Patriot, February 15, 1828, 86; *Halifax Mail*, December 1, 1911, 1. V/F, Vol. 4, No. 3.
Proud Brunswick Street
Acadian Recorder, June 11, 1897, 3.

Impact of Railways

The Nova Scotia Railway

Acadian Recorder, June 17, 1854, 2; *British Colonist*, December 14, 1858, 2; *Daily Sun*, June 14, 1854, 2, February 3, 1855, 2; *Halifax Herald*, June 6, 1893, 1; *Morning Chronicle*, January 3, 1870, 3; *Morning Journal*, June 23, 1854, 2, July 24, 1858, 2; *Times and Courier*, February 10, 1849, 3; *Unionist and Halifax Journal*, June 29, 1866, 2. MG 100, Vol. 157, No. 2.

The Intercolonial Railway

Acadian Recorder, June 1, 1872, November 14, 1872, 2, December 2, 1872, 2, May 13, 1873, 2, February 24, 1875, 3, July 27, 1877, 3, July 28, 1877, 4, August 9, 1877, 3; *Evening Express*, January 9, 1874, 2; *Morning Chronicle*, August 27, 1903, 2, December 30, 1911, 1; *Weekly Citizen*, February 6, 1875, 2. MG 9, Vol. 43, 10; MG 100, Vol. 154, No. 10.

City Railways

Morning Chronicle, January 4, 1867, 3. MG 9, Vol. 225; MG 100, Vol. 159, Nos. 14-14q.

Halifax Harbour Bridges

Acadian Recorder, July 17, 1847, 3; *Morning Chronicle*, February 12, 1885, 3. MG 100, Vol. 153, No. 23.

The Railways Push South

Halifax Herald, December 23, 1918, 1.

Promise of Industry

Richmond Industrializes

Morning Herald, May 16, 1884, 1; *Novascotian*, April 16, 1881, 2, 4, 5, September 21, 1889, 2, 3.

Exhibiting Nova Scotian Industry

Halifax Herald, October 5, 1896, 2, October 23, 1896, 8, May 25, 1897, 1, June 8, 1897, 3, July 27, 1897, 6, September 28, 1897, 8, September 25, 1899, 1, September 12, 1912, 1; *Halifax Mail-Star*, April 30, 1958, 1. MG 100, Vol. 139, No. 35.

The Richmond Community

Chronicle-Herald, April 18, 1959, 4, August 25, 1966, 14; *Halifax Mail-Star*, March 4, 1959, 2.

The Halifax Explosion

Ground Zero

Chronicle-Herald, December 6, 1961, 5; *Halifax Mail-Star*, December 6, 1956, 3. MG 100, Vol. 43, No. 32, Vol. 54, No. 25, Vol. 87, No. 35.

Death and Destruction

Daily News, December 6, 1989, 23, 32; *Chronicle-Herald*, January 31, 1959, 19; *Halifax Evening Mail*, December 10, 1917, 6; *Halifax Herald*, May 21, 1918, 1. MG 100, Vol. 61, No. 90. "Halifax Explosion Remembrance Book." Government of Nova Scotia, http://www.gov.ns.ca/nsarm/virtual/remembrance/ (accessed December 3, 2003).

Rescue and Temporary Relief

"A Vision of Regeneration". Government of Nova Scotia, http://www.gov.ns.ca/nsarm/virtual/explosion/exhibit.asp?ID=26 (accessed December 3, 2003).

Laying Blame

V/F, Vol. 96, No. o.

Explosion Fascination
Mail-Star and Chronicle-Herald, November 1, 2003, c1, c2.

Rebuilding the North End
Temporary Housing
"A Vision of Regeneration." Government of Nova Scotia, http://www.gov.ns.ca/nsarm/virtual/explosion/ (accessed December 15, 2003).
Fort Needham Becomes a Park
Halifax Mail-Star, December 6, 1963, 1; July 22, 1966, 10.

Saga of Africville
Origin and Evolution of Africville
Novascotian, May 25, 1857, 2; *Halifax Mail-Star*, February 18, 1952, 11. MG 1, Vol. 1431, No. 9; MG 100, Vol. 100, No. 44.
Relocation
Halifax Mail-Star, December 18, 1963, 1, December 23, 1963, 4, March 8, 1965, 1, 2, January 12, 1970, 5.
Remembering Africville
Atlantic Baptist, September 15, 1972, 1, 2.

The Second World War
"An East Coast Port"
Halifax Mail-Star, January 16, 1957, 1-5. V/F, Vol. 275, No. 4.
Civilian Defense
Halifax Mail, July 8, 1943, 5. MG 20, Vol. 751, Vol. 753, Vol. 754; RG 35-102, Ser. 34D, D1, D2.
The Second Halifax Explosion
MG 20, Vol. 753.

Urban Renewal
Changing the Face of the North End
Halifax Mail-Star, February 18, 1952, 11. V/F, Vol. 44, No. 1.